Once Upon a Cuento

Bilingual Storytimes in English and Spanish

JAMIE CAMPBELL NAIDOO *and* KATIE SCHERRER

ala
editions

AN IMPRINT OF THE AMERICAN LIBRARY ASSOCIATION
CHICAGO 2016

JAMIE CAMPBELL NAIDOO, PhD, is an endowed associate professor at the University of Alabama School of Library and Information Studies. A former elementary school librarian and children's librarian, he teaches and researches in the areas of library services and programs to diverse populations. Dr. Naidoo has published numerous works on Latino children's literature and librarianship, including the book *Celebrating Cuentos: Promoting Latino Children's Literature and Literacy in Classrooms and Libraries* (Libraries Unlimited, 2010). He is active in REFORMA (The National Association to Promote Library and Information Services to Latinos and the Spanish-Speaking) and ALSC (Association for Library Service to Children).

KATIE SCHERRER is a consultant who specializes in helping libraries and educational organizations adapt to changing community needs. Formerly, as a children's librarian, Ms. Scherrer focused on providing innovative and creative services to diverse populations, particularly first-generation Latino immigrant families. She regularly provides in-person and online training workshops on the topics of library outreach to Latino communities and bilingual storytime programming. She is active in REFORMA (The National Association to Promote Library and Information Services to Latinos and the Spanish-Speaking) and ALSC (Association for Library Service to Children). She received her MLIS from Kent State University in 2009.

© 2016 by the American Library Association

Extensive effort has gone into ensuring the reliability of the information in this book; however, the publisher makes no warranty, express or implied, with respect to the material contained herein.

ISBN: 978-0-8389-1411-3 (paper)

Library of Congress Cataloging-in-Publication Data

Names: Naidoo, Jamie Campbell, author. | Scherrer, Katie, author.
Title: Once upon a cuento : bilingual storytimes in English and Spanish / Jamie Campbell Naidoo and Katie Scherrer.
Description: Chicago : ALA Editions, an imprint of the American Library Association, 2016. | Includes bibliographical references and index.
Identifiers: LCCN 2015043287 | ISBN 9780838914113 (print : alk. paper) Subjects: LCSH: Children's libraries—Activity programs—United States. | Children's libraries—Services to Hispanic Americans. | Education, Bilingual—United States. | Multicultural education—United States.
Classification: LCC Z718.2.U6 N35 2016 | DDC 027.62/51—dc23 LC record available at https://lccn.loc .gov/2015043287

Cover design by Kimberly Thornton. Cover image from *Green Is a Chile Pepper,* © 2014 by Roseanne Greenfield Thong; illustrated by John Parra. Used with permission of Chronicle Books LLC, San Francisco. Visit chroniclebooks.com.

Text design by Alejandra Diaz in the Tisa Pro, Brandon Grotesque and Pacifico typefaces.

♾ This paper meets the requirements of ANSI/NISO Z39.48–1992 (Permanence of Paper).
Printed in the United States of America

20 19 18 17 16   5 4 3 2 1

Contents

Acknowledgments   vii
Introduction   ix

PART I   **GETTING STARTED**

1   Bilingual Programming for Latino
and Spanish-Speaking Children ———————— 3

2   Beginning Outreach to Latino
and Spanish-Speaking Communities ———————— 11

3   Bilingual Storytime When You Do Not Speak Spanish ——— 25

4   Bilingual Storytime: One Program, Many Ways ————— 35

5   Using Digital Media in Bilingual Storytimes ————— 49

PART II   **RESOURCE MATERIALS**

6   Ready-to-Use Bilingual Program Plans ———————— 67

7   Recommended Professional Resources and
Children's Media for Bilingual Programming ————— 133

About the Contributors   147
Index   149

Acknowledgments

This work would not be possible without the help and passion of several dedicated professionals. We wish to thank Maria Lee Goodrich, Beatriz Guevara, Karen Nemeth, and Christian Reynolds for sharing their experiences and expertise working with bilingual children. A special thank-you to our program contributors—Adriana Silva, Mel Trujillo, Kacy Vega, and Kelly Von Zee—for sharing their knowledge and allowing us to publish their engaging program plans. Gracias to Jamie's graduate assistant Alyssa Crisswell for tackling the job of formatting all the entries for chapter 7. Many thanks to Carolina Fernández for her input on the Spanish used in the early literacy messages (chapter 4) and several of the storytime plans (chapter 6). Jamie Santoro at ALA Editions has been extremely gracious and patient throughout the publishing process—thank you!

Our work stands on the shoulders of those who have gone before, blazing the way for library services and collections to all children. We thank all the scholars who taught us what we know about children's literature and public library programming, especially Alma Flor Ada, Joan Atkinson, Annabel Stephens, Saroj Ghoting, Isabel Campoy, and Carolyn Brodie. Thank you to all the passionate librarians and professionals dedicated to connecting Spanish-speaking and Latino children with rich materials in the library, especially Oralia Garza de Cortés, Rose Zertuche Treviño, Irania Macías Patterson, Sandra Ríos Balderrama, Isabel Schon, Lucía González, and Betty Abdmishani. Finally, thank you to all the talented authors, illustrators, musicians, developers, and storytellers who have created the wonderful materials that we can share with the many, diverse children in our bilingual storytimes.

Introduction

SERVING LATINO AND SPANISH-SPEAKING CHILDREN IN THE LIBRARY

he Latino population in the United States represents a vast spectrum of diversity, every bit as unique as that of the American population at large.[1] It can be too easy to generalize about this population, to assume that Spanish-speaking and Latino communities are uniform, with the same informational, recreational, and educational needs. Just as when talking about "millennials" or "children" as one group, some valid information might be gained from generalizations, but librarians often miss the nuances that allow us to truly connect with these individuals if we stop there. Yet, we must start somewhere, and national demographic information can help us begin to get to know the Latino population in the United States.

Latinos are the largest minority group in the United States. According to a 2012 report from the Pew Research Center's Hispanic Trends Project,[2] Hispanics make up 16.9 percent of the total population. More than half (64.5 percent) of Hispanics (10.9 percent of the total population) are born in the United States. The self-described heritage of most Hispanics in the United States (64.2 percent) is Mexican, followed by Puerto Rican (9.3 percent), Cuban (3.7 percent), Salvadoran (3.7 percent), and Dominican (3.1 percent). The concentration of Hispanic origin groups varies by geography. For example, "Mexicans make up 78 percent of Latinos in the Los Angeles area but, in the New York City area, Puerto Ricans (28 percent) and Dominicans (21 percent) are the largest groups. Meanwhile, Salvadorans (32 percent) are most numerous in the Washington, D.C., metro area, and Cubans (54 percent) are the largest group in Miami."[3] The Hispanic population grew at the second-highest rate by race or ethnicity between 2000 and 2012 (50.4 percent), and the majority of that growth (61.9 percent) came from the growth of the native-born Hispanic population. Not only is the Hispanic community the largest minority group in the United States, it is also the youngest, with a median age of just 27, ten years younger than the national median of 37. One-quarter of all newborns in the United States are Hispanic.[4] In seventeen states, at least 20 percent of kindergartners are Latino, up from just eight states in 2000. This change includes states in the Pacific Northwest (Washington, Oregon, and Idaho), the Midwest (Nebraska and Kansas), and the Northeast (Massachusetts, Connecticut, and New Jersey).[5]

There are 37 million Spanish speakers in the United States, making Spanish the most spoken language other than English.[6] Many Latinos, but certainly not all, speak Spanish at home. About 38 percent of Latinos describe themselves as Spanish-dominant, while 36 percent say they are bilingual and 25 percent are English-dominant.[7] These percentages are a little different for younger Latinos, with 36 percent of Latinos ages 16 to 25 describing themselves as English-dominant, 41 percent as bilingual, and 23 percent as Spanish-dominant.[8] Similarly, most (98 percent) native-born Latinos in this age group say they can speak English very well or pretty well, but this ability does not mean abandoning Spanish. When it comes to the children of immigrants, 79 percent of second-generation young people and 38 percent of third generation report proficiency in Spanish. Seventy percent of young Latinos report using Spanglish (a hybrid mix of Spanish and English) when talking with family and friends. Though the exact future of Spanish language use in the United States is impossible to predict, it is very clear from the data available today that the Spanish language, whether in conjunction with other languages or on its own, will continue to play an important role in American society.

LATINO AND SPANISH-SPEAKING CHILDREN IN THE LIBRARY

Why is it important to begin a book on bilingual programming with statistics about Spanish-language usage and Latino population growth? The answer is simple: the landscape of America is changing. People from diverse cultures speaking languages other than English, most often Spanish, are present in almost every city and county throughout the United States. In many places, Spanish-speaking and Latino patrons, particularly first-generation immigrant Latinos, are visiting libraries for the first time. A report from the Pew Research Center on Hispanics and public libraries acknowledges, "When it comes to public libraries, immigrant Hispanics pose both a challenge and an opportunity to the library community."[9] Although librarians in some areas of the country have been offering bilingual or Spanish-language programming for decades, other librarians are faced with the exciting, though somewhat intimidating, prospect of providing these programs for the first time. As the statistics suggest, the Latino and Spanish-speaking populations of one area of the country may be completely different from those in another area. It is important that librarians serving these populations look at census data for their communities to understand which specific Latino cultural groups are represented and then plan the best programs accordingly.

All children need opportunities to hear their language spoken and see their lives validated through engaging cuentos (stories) that reflect their cultural experiences. It is imperative for library programs and material collections to reflect the rich diversity and languages of all the children in the community served by the library.[10] Latino and Spanish-speaking children deserve the best library and literacy programs that include songs, cuentos, rhymes, dichos (proverbs or sayings), books, and digital media celebrating Latino cultural heritage. Providing culturally relevant library materials as well as programs, such as bilingual storytimes, in the first language of a child sends the resounding message that the library cares about Latino and Spanish-speaking families and values the contributions of their cultures to society.

Though very little information is available on library use by Latinos and Spanish speakers, one report did find that most Latinos have a positive perception of the public library.[11] Interestingly, and key for library staff members to keep in mind as they develop outreach strategies, the perceived friendliness of staff was found to have a strong effect on public library use by Latinos, even stronger than access to materials in Spanish. Another report from the Pew Research Center's Hispanic Trends Project also found this strong positive perception among Latinos toward public libraries. Notably, though immigrant Latinos were less likely to have used a public library than were other demographic groups, those who had were the most appreciative of the variety of services the public library offers.[12] Throughout this book we provide suggestions and strategies for librarians interested in welcoming Spanish-speaking and Latino children and their families into the library and greeting them with high-quality customer service, collections, and programs.

ORGANIZATION OF THE BOOK

The book begins with a discussion on the importance of bilingual programming in the lives of Latino and Spanish-speaking children, addressing the unique educational and informational needs of bilingual children. We use the bilingual programs and outreach of pioneer librarian Pura Belpré within the New York Public Library system to frame this discussion. Chapter 2 offers practical suggestions for beginning outreach to Spanish-speaking and Latino communities, emphasizing the importance of relationship-building and community collaboration. This chapter addresses why outreach is needed and profiles a library professional who has had great success engaging Latino families in her rural community.

We follow this discussion of outreach in chapter 3 with suggestions for planning and implementing bilingual storytimes when a librarian does not speak Spanish. This aspect is essential because many librarians who do not speak Spanish are very hesitant to plan bilingual storytimes. The chapter also includes information on selecting bilingual Spanish-English picture books as well as culturally authentic Latino children's books. Chapter 4 describes the various types of bilingual programming available. Specifically, we identify the ways in which the potential goals of a bilingual storytime may impact its design and outline varying styles of using English and Spanish throughout the program. The chapter provides several templates for bilingual storytime design, arranged by specific age groups.

Chapter 5 includes a timely discussion about digital media use by Latino and Spanish-speaking families and addresses the potential of digital apps in library storytimes to meet the multiple literacy needs of bilingual children. We share examples of bilingual digital storybook apps as well as creative apps reinforcing Latino cultural heritage along with commendable literacy and library programs in the United States that incorporate digital media in their service and outreach to Spanish-speaking and Latino families. Considerations for selecting apps to use in bilingual programming are provided as well.

We also include eighteen ready-to-use program plans for bilingual storytimes developed by library professionals with experience working with Spanish-speaking and Latino children. The program plans cover all age groups and include mixed-age and family programs. This feature is particularly important, as many Latino families attend library programming as a unit, and librarians who want to target this population need to develop programs that engage children of multiple ages as well as their adult caregivers. Program plans are arranged by age and theme and include an ending craft or activity, additional suggested materials on the theme, and suggested relevant websites for further exploration.

We conclude with a list of professional materials and online resources to assist you in planning your bilingual storytimes. These resources are accompanied by extensive lists of recommended children's books and songs to use in bilingual programming. Throughout the book we recommend various books, digital apps, music, and other materials for bilingual storytime. As the landscape of bilingual and Spanish-language materials changes, a wonderful and recommended book, digital app, or song may not be available when you are ready to plan a particular themed program. If this is the case, we encourage you to use the sources recommended in the final section as well as the suggestions for evaluating and selecting bilingual books and digital apps to find replacements.

It is our hope that you will find in this book creative ideas, suggestions, and strategies for planning dynamic bilingual storytimes. Katie has used her years of experience working with Latino and Spanish-speaking families to offer suggestions for planning and implementing programs that not only promote literacy development but also celebrate Latino heritage. Her advice has proved valuable to hundreds of librarians who have attended her training workshops. Jamie has also tapped into his experiences working with Latino children's literature, digital apps, and digital picture books and with Latino families to suggest recommendations and guidelines for selecting materials that will motivate and empower Latino and Spanish-speaking children to embrace their culture as they explore the world around them. Together, we have created what we hope is a librarian's toolbox of skills that will jump-start your programming. It should be noted that neither Jamie nor Katie is of Latino heritage, though both have extensive experience working with Latino families in library settings as well as planning and presenting bilingual programs. Every effort has been made to acknowledge and celebrate the diversity of Latino and Spanish-speaking communities and bilingual programming, though our cultural lens undoubtedly impacts our own experience. For this reason, we have included many other voices from across the country who share their expertise in the various aspects of bilingual programming. Many of these professionals are of Latino heritage, and most are affiliated with REFORMA (The National Association to Promote Library and Information Services to Latinos and the Spanish-Speaking).

We encourage you to dare to embrace the rich cultural diversity in your library community! Select the best bilingual and Spanish-language materials for your storytimes. Prepare yourself for a rewarding journey that begins with "Once Upon a Cuento . . ."

NOTES

1. The terms *Latino* and *Hispanic* are often used interchangeably in the United States to refer to the same population of people who either live in or have ancestors in Mexico, Central and South America, Puerto Rico, Cuba, and Spanish-speaking islands in the Caribbean. People who are new immigrants from a Latin American country, U.S. residents of Latin American heritage, and current citizens in a Latin American country are all precariously grouped under these labels. Each term is loaded with social and political implications and is accepted or rejected in various degrees by the people the term purports to represent. Throughout this book readers will find the two terms used interchangeably, depending on the research being cited, though we often opt for the term *Latino*, as it is thought to be more inclusive than the label *Hispanic*. Nonetheless, these labels are used for clarity only. We fully respect the right of all individuals to adopt the term they feel best describes their life experiences, diverse heritage, and unique culture.
2. Anna Brown and Eileen Patten, "Statistical Portrait of Hispanics in the United States, 2012," Pew Research Center (April 29, 2014), www.pewhispanic.org/2014/04/29/statistical-portrait-of-hispanics-in-the-united-states-2012/.
3. Jens Manuel Krogstad, "11 Facts for National Hispanic Heritage Month," Pew Research Center (September 16, 2014), www.pewresearch.org/fact-tank/2014/09/16/11-facts-for-national-hispanic-heritage-month/.
4. Pew Research Center, "Between Two Worlds: How Young Latinos Come of Age in America" (July 1, 2013), www.pewhispanic.org/2009/12/11/between-two-worlds-how-young-latinos-come-of-age-in-america/.
5. Jens Manuel Krogstad, "A View of the Future through Kindergarten Demographics," Pew Research Center (July 8, 2014), www.pewresearch.org/fact-tank/2014/07/08/a-view-of-the-future-through-kindergarten-demographics/.
6. Mark Hugo Lopez and Ana Gonzalez-Barrera, "What Is the Future of Spanish in the United States?" Pew Research Center (September 5, 2013), www.pewresearch.org/fact-tank/2013/09/05/what-is-the-future-of-spanish-in-the-united-states/.
7. Krogstad, "11 Facts for National Hispanic Heritage Month."

8. Pew Research Center, "Between Two Worlds: How Young Latinos Come of Age in America."

9. Anna Brown and Mark Hugo Lopez, "Public Libraries and Hispanics: Immigrant Hispanics Use Libraries Less, But Those Who Do Appreciate Them the Most," Pew Research Center (March 17, 2015), www.pewhispanic.org/2015/03/17/public-libraries -and-hispanics/.

10. Jamie Campbell Naidoo, "The Importance of Diversity in Library Programs and Material Collections for Children," Association for Library Service to Children (April 2014), www.ala.org/alsc/importance-diversity.

11. Edward Flores and Harry Pachon, "Latinos and Public Library Perceptions," Tomás Rivera Policy Institute (September 2008), www.webjunction.org/content/dam/ WebJunction/Documents/webjunction/213544usb_wj_latinos_and_public_library _perceptions.pdf.

12. Brown and Lopez, "Public Libraries and Hispanics."

Part One
GETTING STARTED

Chapter One

Bilingual Programming for Latino and Spanish-Speaking Children

The Board of Education began to appoint Puerto Rican teachers as coordinators in the school system, who helped children preserve their cultural background by means of storytelling and narration of selective materials suitable for their ages. As the public schools joined in the task in which libraries had long been engaged, classes came from the schools for book talks and orientation in Spanish. The library continued its services where requested, going in turn, into the schools to teach library instruction and acquaint children with the public library. By invitation, Puerto Rican mothers, members of the PTA, accompanied classes to the library to see activities offered to the children. After class, the mothers were escorted to the adult department where they could join the library. . . . At one of the libraries a mother discovering a collection of Spanish books exclaimed, "Come my children, quench your thirst."[1]

lthough it reads almost like a storybook excerpt, the preceding passage recounts events that occurred once upon a time in a public library in New York City in the 1960s. Spanish-speaking and Latino children and their families enjoyed bilingual storytimes, puppet shows, and other library programs infused with beautiful Spanish-language and culturally rich stories representing diverse Latino cultures from Puerto Rico, Cuba, Mexico, and beyond. Through the work of several dedicated children's librarians such as Ernestine Rose, Anne Carroll Moore, Mary Gould Davis, and Augusta Baker, decades of Spanish-speaking and Latino children throughout New York City reaped the rewards of the outreach efforts of library pioneer Pura Belpré. Collectively, these women empowered Belpré, the first Puerto Rican librarian in the New York Public Library system, to offer innovative bilingual storytimes and outreach programming to thousands of Spanish-speaking children.

Through Belpré's programs, children made important literacy connections with printed books and oral stories while seeing their language and culture celebrated in the library.[2]

Although many of these magical encounters occurred more than fifty years ago, contemporary librarians can look to the work of Belpré as they consider their library's services to Latino and Spanish-speaking children and their families. The key is to provide opportunities for these children to encounter their language and culture in library programs such as the bilingual storytime and to make the library welcoming and accessible for all families. Reinforcing many of the ideas behind the bilingual programs developed by Belpré, this chapter describes the role of language in the Latino child's development, underscores the importance of offering culturally relevant bilingual storytimes, and explores common myths related to Spanish-language literacy instruction and activities.

LANGUAGE AND LITERACY DEVELOPMENT OF LATINO CHILDREN

Language influences identity development and is an inherent part of every child's culture. Young children rapidly develop new social, cognitive, and linguistic skills in their first three years of life. When children live in an environment that supports their language, they are free to explore, learn, and grow into lifelong learners. They can use print and digital media, their daily experiences, and their immediate contexts to better understand their place in the world and develop a sense of self.

For children growing up speaking a language other than English at home, it is important to have meaningful early literacy experiences in the home language. These experiences first and foremost support home language acquisition, an essential key for family communication and an integral part of cultural identity. Decades of research indicate that children learn best in their home language and that literacy encounters in a child's first language can support the development of a second language.[3]

Children whose first language is not English are faced with two challenges upon entering school: acquiring English as well as learning skills and gaining knowledge through English-language instruction.[4] If a child is not fluent in English, he cannot acquire the necessary information to advance in the U.S. educational system. Children who have a strong foundation of early literacy in their home language have an easier time learning a second language, such as English, than do those who have had less language exposure. Literacy instruction and activities in the home language of a child support cognitive development, encourage self-esteem, enhance social interactions, and strengthen family ties.[5] When young children are forced to abandon their first language for a new language, they essentially begin the literacy process without any prior background knowledge to support their emergent literacy in the new language. As a result, children perceive a disconnect between their home and school environments, which can lead to feelings of frustration and inadequacy.[6] Their self-esteem begins to drop as they fall behind their native-English-speaking peers and learn that Spanish is considered subpar to English.

IMPORTANCE OF OFFERING CULTURALLY RELEVANT BILINGUAL STORYTIMES

Why offer a storytime in Spanish or bilingually in English and Spanish? Before passage of the Bilingual Education Act of 1968 and the bilingual amendment to the Elementary and Secondary Education Act of 1965, many Spanish-speaking children in the United States had few opportunities to encounter their home language in library and instructional materials, much less engage in language and literacy activities in Spanish. Although a few exemplary bilingual programs could be found in public libraries, such as those given by Pura Belpré at the New York Public Library from the 1920s through the 1940s and from 1960 to 1978, little attention was given to offering library programs for children either bilingually or in Spanish.

The preschool storytime has been used by public libraries for decades to socialize young children and connect them with high-quality literature. Within the past ten years, early literacy storytimes have become more common in libraries to help preschoolers develop emergent literacy skills and to educate parents on how to foster language development. Storytime is also the perfect place to connect with Latino and Spanish-speaking children. The use of Spanish during a bilingual storytime reinforces the perception that the library values the language and supports the cognitive and social development of Spanish-speaking children. Librarians who offer bilingual storytimes can build a bridge between the home and school cultures experienced by Latino and Spanish-speaking children. Spanish-language stories, rhymes, poems, and songs affirm and validate the language and culture of these children and their families.

A well-planned bilingual storytime enhances a child's literacy development by providing a meaningful, engaging approach to emergent literacy. Bilingual or Spanish-language cuentos (stories), dichos (sayings), and songs offer rich context and meaning through familiar words and phrases from a child's home language. As we will discuss later, high-quality children's books that mirror the home environments of Latino and Spanish-speaking children are ideal for validating a child's culture and heritage. Collectively, these materials, used within the context of bilingual storytime, affirm a child's language and culture and significantly help in the formation of a Latino child's ethnic identity development.

But I Don't Speak Spanish

Although you may have a strong passion for serving Latino and Spanish-speaking children, you may find the task daunting. Often, librarians who do not speak Spanish or who know little about Latino cultures list these insufficiencies as obstacles to providing bilingual storytime and outreach to these families. As we discuss later in this book, you can offer dynamic service and bilingual storytimes to Latino and Spanish-speaking families by using the ingenuity and creativity in your librarian's toolbox of skills to help you connect everyone in the community with the wonderful resources in your library. Former outreach librarian Lillian López, who worked with Pura Belpré, offers reassuring advice to librarians serving diverse cultures: "The two words, love and trust, are among the most beautiful in the English language. When you serve with sincerity, people are going to trust you regardless of your ethnic background. A child can always tell when you are sincere."[7]

In other words, do not let perceived roadblocks or fear hinder you from reaching out to Latino and Spanish-speaking children and families in your community. Rather, collaborate with other organizations serving these families or work with Spanish-speaking educators and parents to help you plan your programs and services. Seek Latino and Spanish-speaking partners to assist you with bilingual storytimes and, most important, remember that your bilingual programs do not have to be confined to the four walls of your physical library building. Bilingual storytimes can be offered in playgrounds, community centers, churches, parks, schools, day care centers, and Head Start programs frequented by Spanish-speaking children and their families.

Why Should I Use Latino Children's Materials in Storytime?

Culturally authentic children's books can be highly influential in assisting young Latino children as they develop their ethnic identities and make connections between their home culture and the larger educational culture found in schools and libraries. Research indicates that children's materials with Latino characters and themes can have either a positive or negative impact upon the self-esteem and identity development of young Latinos.[8] A picture book that authentically captures the nuances of a particular Latino subculture and accurately depicts daily experiences can reinforce the self-esteem of Latino children and validate their existence. For non-Latino children, the book can also serve as a window into the lives of their friends or classmates, creating a bridge of understanding. However, if an informational book portrays Latino characters as poor, dirty, or unintelligent, then Latino children are likely to be embarrassed by their culture, and non-Latino children may develop cultural stereotypes about Latinos.

Equally harmful to the ethnic identity development and self-esteem of Latino and Spanish-speaking children is the complete absence from library collections and storytimes of books that reflect their cultural experiences. When a child never encounters her culture or daily experiences in the library, then she receives a resounding message that the library thinks she is unimportant or insignificant. Latino children's book creators such as René Colato Laínez and Maya Christina Gonzalez have described experiencing feelings of inadequacy during their childhood because of the absence of Spanish-speaking, bilingual, or Latino characters in the books they read in school or encountered in the library. Both of these authors have made a concerted effort to urge educators and librarians to include Latino children's books and other materials in the curriculum to assist Latino children with their identity development.

MYTHS RELATED TO SPANISH-LANGUAGE LITERACY INSTRUCTION AND ACTIVITIES

When you plan bilingual storytimes or library programs in Spanish, you may face resistance from fellow librarians, administrators, local government officials, or community members. It is important to know how to respond effectively to any concerns and to reinforce the mission of the library to serve everyone in the community. In this section, we present some common misperceptions or myths related to offering Spanish-language or bilingual programs to children, along with facts that debunk those myths.

MYTH 1 A Spanish-speaking child's language development in English can become delayed if a librarian or other educator offers bilingual English-Spanish literacy instruction or library programs.

FACT Each child is unique in his language development. Although there may be observable delays or lapses at particular stages in development, research indicates that second-language acquisition is actually enhanced when a child receives instruction in his first language.[9] Bilingual instruction reinforces language development in both languages.

MYTH 2 The best way to help young children learn a new language is immersion, with all books, instruction, playful interactions (such as singing), and conversations in the new language.

FACT Young children need continuous learning support in the home language to provide a solid foundation for acquiring a new language. Children should have equal opportunities to interact with materials and to engage in literacy activities in both the home and new languages.[10]

MYTH 3 Bilingual storytimes or literacy activities will confuse young native English speakers and inhibit their successful literacy development.

FACT When native English speakers are exposed continuously to a second language such as Spanish through bilingual instruction, their English literacy development is equally enhanced.[11] Like their non-native English-speaking counterparts, they too have the opportunity to begin acquiring a new language—Spanish in this instance. In fact, many librarians who offer bilingual Spanish-English storytimes report that attendance by native English speakers is equal to, and often greater than, that of Spanish speakers.

MYTH 4 Providing bilingual instruction or bilingual storytimes is expensive and a drain on resources for English-speaking children.

FACT Bilingual and Spanish books and materials do not cost more than English-language books. The acquisition of bilingual Spanish-English books and music CDs enhances both the English-language and Spanish-language collections. Moreover, both monolingual and bilingual storytimes require careful and purposeful planning. Although some aspects of planning for a new bilingual storytime may take more of an initial time investment than planning for a new monolingual storytime, that time investment is often required because the organization's current services to Latino and Spanish-speaking families are lacking, not because bilingual storytime is inherently more time-consuming. By making an appropriate time investment up front to ensure the program effectively reaches and engages Spanish-speaking families, the library is coming closer to ensuring its mission of providing equal access to all of its community.

A particularly useful resource for librarians who confront resistance to the library offering bilingual and Spanish-language storytimes is Linda Espinosa's "Challenging Common Myths about Young English Language Learners."[12] This brief report explores several myths about language acquisition and Latino cultural values and provides research-based information to debunk these myths. You can use this resource when responding to concerns.

CONCLUDING THOUGHTS

All children need opportunities to hear their language spoken and to encounter book characters reflective of their cultural heritage. The public library that is offering vibrant, developmentally appropriate bilingual storytimes holds significant potential for connecting with Latino and Spanish-speaking children and their families. Almost fifty years ago, children's librarian Toni de Gerez surmised, "The earlier a child is exposed to books in both English and Spanish, the sooner he will feel at home in both cultures. He will enjoy 'exploring' even when he may know little or nothing of one language, and his confidence in one will carry over to the other. Once he is no longer ashamed of the language he speaks at home, he will move with pride and dignity."[13] By providing rich opportunities for all families to encounter children's literature and literacy activities in both Spanish and English, the library can be a place where pride and dignity indeed flourish.

NOTES

1. Pura Belpré White, "A Bilingual Story Hour Program," *Library Journal* 89 (September 15, 1964), 28–29.

2. For additional information on the work of Belpré, consult Lisa Sánchez González, ed., *The Stories I Read to the Children: The Life and Writing of Pura Belpré, the Legendary Storyteller, Children's Author, and New York Public Librarian* (New York: Center for Puerto Rican Studies, Hunter College SUNY, 2013).

3. Sonia Nieto, *Language, Culture, and Teaching: Critical Perspectives for a New Century* (Mahwah, NJ: Erlbaum, 2002); Costanza Eggers-Piérola, *Connections and Commitments: Reflecting Latino Values in Early Childhood Programs* (Portsmouth, NH: Heinemann, 2005); Eugene E. García and Erminda H. García, *Understanding the Language Development and Early Education of Hispanic Children* (New York: Teachers College Press, 2012).

4. Guadalupe Valdés, Sarah Capitelli, and Laura Alvarez, *Latino Children Learning English: Steps in the Journey* (New York: Teachers College Press, 2011).

5. Karen N. Nemeth, *Basics of Supporting Dual Language Learners: An Introduction for Educators of Children from Birth through Age 8* (Washington, DC: National Association for the Education of Young Children, 2012).

6. Rosa Hernández Sheets, *Diversity Pedagogy: Examining the Role of Culture in the Teaching-Learning Process* (Boston: Pearson Education, 2005); Katherine H. Au, *Literacy Instruction in Multicultural Settings* (Fort Worth, TX: Harcourt Brace College, 1993).

7. Lillian López with Pura Belpré, "Reminiscences of Two Turned-On Librarians," in *Puerto Rican Perspectives,* ed. Edward Mapp (Metuchen, NJ: Scarecrow Press, 1974), 93.

8. Ellen Riojas Clark, Belinda Bustos Flores, Howard L. Smith, and Daniel Alejandro González, eds., *Multicultural Literature for Latino Bilingual Children: Their Words, Their Worlds* (Lanham, MD: Rowman and Littlefield, 2015); Jamie Naidoo, ed., *Celebrating Cuentos: Promoting Latino Children's Literature and Literacy in Classrooms and Libraries* (Santa Barbara, CA: Libraries Unlimited, 2011); Alma Flor Ada, *A Magical Encounter: Latino Children's Literature in the Classroom,* 2nd ed. (Boston: Allyn and Bacon, 2003).

9. Nieto, *Language, Culture, and Teaching;* Sheets, *Diversity Pedagogy;* Valdés, Capitelli, and Alvarez, *Latino Children Learning English;* Eggers-Piérola, *Connections and Commitments.*

10. Nieto, *Language, Culture, and Teaching;* Sheets, *Diversity Pedagogy;* Valdés, Capitelli, and Alvarez, *Latino Children Learning English;* Eggers-Piérola, *Connections and Commitments.*

11. Nieto, *Language, Culture, and Teaching;* Sheets, *Diversity Pedagogy;* Valdés, Capitelli, and Alvarez, *Latino Children Learning English;* Eggers-Piérola, *Connections and Commitments.*

12. Linda M. Espinosa, "Challenging Common Myths about Young English Language Learners," Foundation for Child Development Policy Brief 8 (January 2008), http://fcd-us.org/sites/default/files/MythsOfTeachingELLsEspinosa.pdf.

13. Toni de Gerez, "Books for Miguel," *School Library Journal* 92 (December 15, 1967), 46.

Chapter Two

Beginning Outreach to Latino and Spanish-Speaking Communities

t is impossible to talk about planning and implementing bilingual storytime programming without first talking about outreach to Latino communities. Too often, when well-meaning librarians realize that their Spanish-speaking communities are growing and their library is not keeping pace with the change, they decide to implement a bilingual or Spanish-language storytime program as a first step toward closing this service gap. Storytime is something libraries understand and know how to do well. Though it may push library staff members out of their comfort zone to offer storytime in another language, it is still well within the realm of traditional service. However, when it comes to serving Latino and Spanish-speaking communities, bilingual storytime is neither a panacea nor an inherently "if you build it, they will come" type of program. For a bilingual or Spanish-language storytime program to make an impact, it is critical to first build the foundation of library service to the targeted community through strategic outreach.

WHY IS OUTREACH NECESSARY?

Quite often when libraries decide to offer a bilingual or Spanish-language storytime program, they are hoping to attract families from the Spanish-speaking community who are not yet library users. Without a strong foundation of outreach already in place, however, a bilingual storytime on its own is not likely to be enough to draw new families to the library. Organizations that are successfully engaging with the Latino community likely do the following:

- Have bilingual and bicultural staff at various positions and levels of responsibility throughout the organization
- Actively participate in community groups that work to meet various needs of the Spanish-speaking community in the region or area
- Have a culturally relevant Spanish-language collection that circulates well and responds to the wants and needs of the community being served
- Maintain creative partnerships with local agencies that work to address informational, financial, health, legal, and other needs
- Have strong relationships with the local Latino media in all forms

Those whose organizations fit the preceding description can likely skip the outreach section of this book, because they already have ongoing outreach and service responses integrated at an institutional level. They are likely well on their way to establishing the audience they want to reach with the bilingual storytime program and are now looking for practical suggestions on how to develop or improve this program. However, organizations not already doing this foundational work may be starting to see the work that lies ahead.

There are numerous reasons why the Latino community in the area may be underserved. Depending on the diversity (or lack thereof, presently or in the past) of the frontline staff, management, administration, or board, the growth of this community may not have been noticed. Perhaps the organization tried to respond to the growing community in misguided ways that were not well received, such as purchasing Spanish-language versions of American best sellers. When such attempts at service did not reach traditional standards of success (such as strong circulation numbers), organization members may have become disheartened: "We tried purchasing Spanish-language books once, but they didn't circulate, so now we don't buy them anymore." Maybe the organization had some success at the individual level but failed to integrate that success institutionally. For example, hiring a specific bilingual, bicultural outreach person can be an excellent step in building relationships and trust, but there is the risk that such a measure leads to regarding service to the Spanish-speaking community as the work of only one person or department rather than the organization as a whole. If this outreach person leaves or the department changes, the relationships that were built may fade away. Regardless of why the community has been underserved, the organization has to honestly contend with the fact that the community is underserved today. Though it is important to understand any factors that may have contributed to this lack of service, it is also important not to get stuck navel-gazing or assigning blame. The objective is to ensure that the organization is making real progress toward full inclusion of the Latino community going forward from today. Librarians may harbor several myths about serving Latino or Spanish-speaking populations, and figure 2.1 suggests points to consider that will help debunk three of these myths.

The specific reasons why Latinos and Spanish speakers are not using the library will vary from area to area. There may not be a history of library use in the family. If you are serving recent immigrants, public library services might not have been available in their home countries. Even if the community is familiar

---

FIGURE 2.1

LATINOS AND LIBRARY USE

▶ **Common Myths and Questions for Reflection**

MYTH 1 **Latinos do not visit the library.**
What efforts has the organization made to ensure that the library space and staff are inclusive and welcoming?

MYTH 2 **Latinos don't know what resources are available at the library.**
What has the organization done to spread this information through the communication channels regularly used by the community?

MYTH 3 **Latinos do not value the library and its resources.**
How is the organization ensuring that the collection and programs address the specific information and entertainment needs of the Latino community?

---

with libraries and enjoys reading for pleasure, members may not be aware of the many other programs and services traditionally offered by libraries in the United States, such as storytime. Community members might have misunderstandings about the cost of library services or the security of personal information. They might fear being unable to communicate with staff and being embarrassed (particularly in front of children) because of a language barrier. Whatever the reasons, the library has a responsibility to identify the barriers that are blocking access and to make efforts to overcome these barriers. This is done in a radically old-fashioned way—by getting out of the library building and meeting people, one at a time.

THE OUTREACH PROCESS

In this section we do not intend to present an exhaustive guide to library outreach to the Latino community. Other, highly recommended resources are available that can walk you through the process of launching an outreach initiative that specifically targets Latinos and Spanish speakers. Figure 2.2 provides a list of these recommended resources. Rather, this section presents basic first steps that any organization considering a bilingual or Spanish-language storytime program should be willing to undertake in order to engage with the community in a meaningful way and to set up the new program for success.

1. **Research the local Latino and Spanish-speaking community.** National demographic data about the Latino community was presented in chapter 1. Research similar data for your local area. The U.S. Census Bureau's American FactFinder (http://factfinder.census.gov) and the Pew Research Center's Hispanic Trends Project (www.pewhispanic.org) are good places to start.

FIGURE 2.2

BEGINNING OUTREACH TO LATINO AND SPANISH-SPEAKING COMMUNITIES

▶ **Recommended Resources**

Alire, Camila, and Jacqueline Ayala. *Serving Latino Communities: A How-to-Do-It Manual for Librarians.* 2nd ed. New York: Neal-Schuman, 2007.

Avila, Salvador. *Crash Course in Serving Spanish-Speakers.* Westport, CT: Libraries Unlimited, 2008.

Baumann, Susana. *¡Hola, amigos! A Plan for Latino Outreach.* Santa Barbara, CA: Libraries Unlimited, 2011.

Breiseth, Lydia. "A Guide for Engaging ELL Families: Twenty Strategies for School Leaders." ¡Colorín Colorado! (August 2011), www.colorincolorado.org/pdfs/guides/Engaging-ELL-Families.pdf.

Byrd, Susannah. *¡Bienvenidos! ¡Welcome! A Handy Resource Guide for Marketing Your Library to Latinos.* Chicago: American Library Association, 2005.

REFORMA: The National Association to Promote Library and Information Services to Latinos and the Spanish-Speaking, www.reforma.org/.

WebJunction. "Spanish Language Outreach Program," www.webjunction.org/explore-topics/slo.html.

Consider also your state's data center, major universities, economic development groups, and the chamber of commerce. This research should be ongoing, and as you make new relationships within the community, the data will continually be refined. Think of the data collection process as circular rather than linear: by learning realistic and accurate information about the community, you will be able to develop better strategies for launching relevant and well-received services. Figure 2.3 provides some useful questions to consider when beginning to research demographics in your local community.

2. **Interview community leaders.** To best serve Latinos and Spanish speakers in your area, it is critical to look beyond the numbers. The community leader interview is invaluable for your research. From 2004 to 2008, WebJunction offered a series of professional development workshops to help librarians across the country learn to better connect with growing Spanish-speaking communities.[1] From those workshops comes one of the best tools for beginning to learn about and build relationships with the Latino community—the community leader interview. Trusted community leaders act as a gateway for reaching underserved families. These leaders may or may not be in formal positions of leadership; they may be teachers, pastors, health-care professionals, receptionists, volunteers, child-care providers, or business leaders. It is not uncommon that the people in frontline positions have the most direct contact with Latino families and will thus be more useful in practical terms than the people in more authoritative positions of power. It is helpful to identify three to five community leaders to begin with and reach out to them to set up an interview. Use a personal touch; calling people individually or even dropping by their office is likely to be met with a more

---

FIGURE 2.3

BEGINNING OUTREACH TO LATINO AND SPANISH-SPEAKING COMMUNITIES

▶ **Research Questions**

- What community does the library want to serve with this program? If that community is one of immigrants, what is known about their countries of origin and home cultures?
- What are the day-to-day lives like of the families the library wants to reach? Are specific industries or employers drawing the community to this area?
- Are certain areas of town experiencing larger growth in the community than others? Why?
- What are the needs of this community (informational, educational, health, entertainment, legal, etc.)? What other agencies and organizations are working to meet these needs? What needs are currently not being met?

---

positive response than is sending an e-mail, even though calling or stopping by requires investing more time. Be willing to go to these leaders rather than asking them to come to the library for the interview. Explain that you are trying to learn more about the Latino and Spanish-speaking community in order to provide better service. Have a prepared set of questions (not too many—remember that these leaders may be quite busy), but be willing to go off script to delve into the unique perspective of each community leader. End every interview by asking the leader to recommend others you could contact; this technique will help you build a network. Follow up with a thank-you note, and keep each leader apprised of the library's progress from time to time. The "Community Leader Interview Guide" developed by Yolanda Cuesta walks library staff through the process, providing great tips on how to identify community leaders, how to set up the interview, and what kinds of questions to ask.[2] A sample interview is provided in the guide as well.

3. **Take the library to the community.** The information gathered in the previous steps has allowed you to learn more *about* the Latino community. Now it is time for you and your library to engage *with* the Latino community. Using the information you discovered regarding the organizations and businesses the Latino community frequents and about the informational needs of the community, prepare a "library road show" and go meet families where they are. Include the following:
   - *Someone who is bilingual in English and Spanish.* Ideally this person is a bicultural staff member who is being well compensated for his or her time. However, the person may be a staff member who is bilingual but not bicultural or even a volunteer. The person might work with one of the library's partner agencies that is serving the Latino community. Whomever you select, the person must be approachable and friendly, must understand how the library works and what it has to offer, and must be able to communicate with Spanish speakers with ease.

- *Relevant resources.* What did you discover in your research about informational and entertainment needs? What does the library have that addresses these needs? Select materials that show what the library has to offer. These materials may be books, of course, but you may also include Spanish-language flyers for upcoming programs, a demonstration of the storytime program, or a Spanish-language video introduction to the library that plays on a tablet. Bring resources that are relevant and interesting. Be creative! However, even a very simple approach (a person and some books) can be effective. The most critical thing is to put a human face on the library and establish connections.

Take your library road show to local Latino networking groups or the Hispanic Chamber of Commerce; English for Speakers of Other Languages (ESOL) classes; local day-care centers; and community events and information fairs well attended by the community you are trying to reach, such as Latino holiday celebrations, sporting events, information fairs, or school festivals.

4. **Follow up.** Outreach is an ongoing process, and it requires regular external and internal follow-up. External follow-up means regularly touching base with community contacts and leaders. This is an important part of maintaining good relationships and truly becoming a trusted part of the community. Being connected will also help the library to stay aware of changing community needs and challenges. The organization should make efforts to ensure that Latino community leaders are represented in positions on the board of trustees or other advisory groups. Consider establishing a panel of Latino Service Advisors who help guide the organization in its ongoing outreach efforts. Internal follow-up means being an advocate within the organization to ensure that all aspects of service are inclusive of Latinos and Spanish speakers. Progress should be regularly shared with supervisors, administrators, and colleagues using any available channels, such as staff intranet or newsletters, management meetings, and even informal conversations. The work of connecting the library and the Latino community is that of the entire organization, not just one person or department, so it is important to proactively communicate both the successes and shortcomings throughout the process. Figure 2.4 presents three additional tips for staff providing outreach that targets the Latino and Spanish-speaking community.

5. **Ensure the library is a welcoming space.** The spirit of outreach continues inside the library walls as well. One bad interaction with unfriendly or hostile staff can undermine all the effort and time put into your outreach initiative. Imagine how frustrating and disheartening it would be to be encouraged to visit a place, only to be treated as though you were not welcome there once you arrived. One librarian (who wished to remain anonymous) recalls this incident:

One of our frontline staff noticed a woman who appeared to be Latina looking confused on the computer. She approached the woman and in an annoyed tone asked, "What do you need?" The woman just looked at her and did not reply. The staff person then approached me and told me there was someone at the computer who needed help who did not speak English and that I needed to go help her in Spanish. When I approached the woman, she was understandably furious. "I actually speak three languages, including English. I gave her that look because I thought she was being incredibly rude in how she approached me." This staff person's assumptions about Latinos came through in her interaction with this customer. It was eye-opening in terms of what kinds of changes we needed to make among our staff.[3]

FIGURE 2.4

OUTREACH TIPS

TIP 1   Get comfortable with being uncomfortable!

For a lot of people, working with a different culture puts them outside their comfort zone. Even with the best intentions, people may feel nervous, worry about not understanding common cultural nuances, fear making mistakes when using a different language, and more. Try to move past these nerves and reach out anyway! People who don't speak English very well or who are new to this country feel this way too, and most are very appreciative of any efforts to make an organization more inclusive and welcoming. Use common sense, be respectful, learn from mistakes, and go for it!

TIP 2   Know your organization!

What organizational supports exist to improve library services to Latinos and Spanish speakers, such as staff time, budget, and the like? How does this work connect to the strategic goals and values of the organization? Does the administration respond best to data and figures or would anecdotes and stories be more effective? It is possible to find yourself having to advocate up the chain of authority at times. By knowing how the organization intends to assess the effectiveness of the outreach program, you can know the appropriate data to collect along the way.

TIP 3   Cultivate trust!

Perhaps the most subtle yet also the most profound element to successfully working with Latinos and Spanish speakers is trust. This observation is more than anecdotal—a 2012 Pew Research Center report found that levels of personal trust among Latinos are much lower than levels among the general population: "Fully 86% of Latinos say you can't be too careful when it comes to dealing with people. Among the U.S. general public, just 61% say the same."[1] Librarians may not tend to think that a personal relationship with a trusted library staff member is an essential part of access. Sure, customers develop relationships with individual librarians and staff, but if they arrive on a day when their favorite person is not working, they will still go up to someone else and get the help that they need. In this mental model of library service, the expectation is that customers trust the institution of the public library. However, when working with Spanish speakers (particularly first-generation immigrants and those who are not yet library users), it is important to be aware that they may not have an inherent trust in the institution of the library. Such trust must be cultivated first through establishing personal relationships and then by working to transfer that trust from the personal level to the institutional. This is a different framework and approach to service, and it takes time to build.

NOTE

1. Paul Taylor, Mark Hugo Lopez, Jessica Martínez, and Gabriel Velasco, "When Labels Don't Fit: Hispanics and Their Views of Identity," Pew Research Center (April 4, 2012), www.pewhispanic.org/2012/04/04/when-labels-dont-fit-hispanics-and-their-views-of-identity.

Staff at all levels must be held to standards of culturally competent, quality customer service for all people. This expectation is particularly critical when serving the Latino community. A 2008 study on Latino public library perceptions by the Tomás Rivera Policy Institute found that "Latinos are more concerned with friendly staff service than Spanish language access."[4] One way to assess your baseline status in terms of the degree of welcome your library exudes is to ask the community leaders you are meeting in your outreach work to do a library walk-through and to give you honest feedback on their experience. Have a plan of action in place for all staff members that empowers them to serve customers who speak languages other than English in a friendly, efficient way. Finally, hold staff members accountable if they refuse to comply with this standard of professionalism; such behavior simply cannot be acceptable.

MARKETING AND ADVERTISING TO LATINOS AND SPANISH SPEAKERS

The terms *marketing* and *advertising* are often used interchangeably, though they actually refer to different but related functions. Marketing is systemic and ongoing; it includes customer (and potential customer) research, program design, promotion, distribution, and outcomes assessment. Advertising is one small, though important, piece of the overall marketing strategy. All of what has previously been presented (identifying the community, learning about informational needs, making contact with community leaders, having a presence at trusted locations, etc.) could be considered part of an organizational marketing strategy. Doing the research, engaging in outreach, and building relationships are all part of how to market the library to Latinos and Spanish speakers. How to get the word out to your prospective audience is advertising.

Libraries often advertise through their website and flyers. They may go a step further and distribute those flyers to local agencies and schools and promote upcoming events on social media. But these regularly used channels are not likely to be sufficient for reaching Spanish speakers who are not currently library users. The following are some specific advertising suggestions.

- **Translate promotional materials into Spanish.** Posting flyers and making website announcements, even when they are in Spanish, is not enough, but it is a start. If the library has Spanish-speaking staff members, they may be able to translate some documents in-house, though this work does go beyond most basic job requirements and staff members should be appropriately compensated for their time and skills. If in-house translation is not an option, look for creative partnership opportunities in the community (i.e., partnering with an advanced Spanish-language class at a university). It may be necessary to budget funds to outsource translations. Figure 2.5 provides suggestions on how to translate "bilingual storytime" in a meaningful way.

FIGURE 2.5

BILINGUAL STORYTIME

▶ **What's in a Name?**

The word *storytime* has many connotations in English. For parents, the word often invokes memories of the library from their childhood and is understood to be a part of how they prepare their own child for school success. The term storytime means something beyond just the literal meaning of the word. This implied meaning may be lost with a literal translation of storytime, such as Tiempo de cuentos. For families who do not have a history of attending storytime, this translation may sound too stiff. Families may think the program requires being very quiet and still. They may be concerned that their child is too active and might become bored or cause a distraction. Consider giving the program a title that is less focused on stories and reading and that implies more about what contemporary storytime actually is, such as Bebés Juguetones (Playful Babies), Juega y Aprende (Play and Learn), or ¡Colorín Colorado! (a phrase Spanish speakers will recognize that is often used at the end of storytelling).

- **Reach out to Spanish-language media**. In many cities, even small markets, there may be Spanish-language television stations, newspapers, or radio stations. Often such media focus on local information and would love to help spread the word about the library. Meeting first with someone from the local media for a community leader interview is a great way not only to further market research but also to begin a relationship that may improve access to local media. As relationships are built, natural opportunities will emerge. Maybe the newspaper is willing to translate press releases to Spanish for publication. The paper may have an events calendar where the library can list upcoming programs. Perhaps the radio or television station would be willing to feature library staff as guests. Don't let a lack of Spanish-speaking staff prevent outreach to Spanish-language media; potential partnerships cannot emerge without first starting the conversation. As is the case for the general population, access to smart phones and the use of social media are changing how Latinos gather and share information. Do not forget to promote library services relevant to Latinos through social media in addition to traditional media. Depending on the community and the resources available, the library may want to consider creating YouTube videos, Facebook events, and tweets about the library in Spanish.

- **Connect with Latino networking agencies.** Working with Latino networking agencies can be quite effective for making contacts, learning about the general needs of the Latino community, learning what resources are currently available to the community, and promoting library services to trusted community leaders who are working with Latinos every day. Networking groups may exist as nonprofit organizations; networking meetings may also be part of the services offered by organizations dedicated to serving Latinos and Spanish speakers on a variety of needs, such as education, adult skills training, and civic engagement. Networking groups are generally made up of one or two representatives from various community agencies and businesses that specifically provide services to the Latino community or that are trying to better connect their general services with the Latino community. Examples of the types of agencies represented are churches, health departments, doctors' offices and clinics, lawyers' offices, school systems, early childhood educators, colleges, Latino media, small businesses, and more. Networking agencies may meet regularly in person, such as once a month or once a quarter. They may have online resources as well, such as websites, electronic discussion lists, community event calendars, and databases of community resources. Meetings may include a speaker on a specific topic relevant to local community issues, as well as time for informal networking. Be sure to bring business cards as well as any flyers or promotional materials for library services or upcoming programs. Networking groups are a great place for meeting community leaders to interview later. The structure, organization, and formality of networking groups will vary greatly from town to town. Some may have little or no online presence. Some towns may not have any networking groups currently established. In such a case, consider inviting representatives from such organizations as those listed earlier to get together for at least one meeting. It may be surprising what can be discovered when multiple stakeholders have the opportunity to discuss shared challenges and solutions.

OUTREACH IN ACTION CASE STUDY

ADRIANA SILVA

When Adriana Silva was first hired as youth services associate at the Florence Branch of the Boone County (Kentucky) Public Library in 2008, the management knew that the Spanish-speaking community was growing, but there had not yet been any outreach specifically targeting this relatively new community. It was obvious that Adriana, born and raised in Mexico and a native Spanish speaker, would be able to help the library better serve this community in some way. The resulting journey makes for an amazing case study in responsive customer service and relationship-building.

When Adriana was first hired, she was new to her job, new to the area, and new to the library profession. But her team was eager for her to hit the ground running. She was hired in the spring, and the team immediately wanted her to present a Cinco de Mayo program. "It was terrible," she recalls, laughing. "It was my first library program, and I had no idea what to do. I also didn't yet know how to reach out to the Hispanic community, so no Hispanic families attended." Gradually she began to learn more about the community of mostly first-generation immigrants from Mexico and Guatemala, drawn to Kentucky for work in the horse industry as well as construction and landscaping. At first, men were arriving on their own. Over time, they began to feel secure enough to bring their families and truly establish their lives in the area; this change has mostly happened within the past ten to fifteen years.

Originally, library management envisioned that Adriana would help provide customer service to Spanish speakers inside the library, in addition to her youth services work. Therefore, she wasn't going outside the library walls much in the beginning. However, not many people were coming to the library for her to help. Any programs she launched to target this community flopped. Over time she began to make connections with important community leaders, the key people Spanish speakers in the community trusted and turned to for help as they settled into small-town Kentucky life.

The first and most important contact that allowed Adriana to start connecting with Latino families was the school system. As more children who spoke Spanish began entering the district, the school found itself facing new challenges, particularly as there were no bilingual staff members at the time. Teachers in the school knew of Adriana and began asking her for help. She presented bilingual storytime in kindergarten classrooms. She attended Family Reading Nights and talked to families about the library. She attended kindergarten registration and helped Spanish-speaking families complete the (English-only) paperwork. She came to back-to-school events and spoke with families in Spanish; their eyes would light up when they heard her, because being able to communicate in their preferred language with anyone representing a community agency was rare indeed.

Adriana's philosophy for serving the Latino community in Boone County is really centered on saying yes whenever she can, not only to individual customers but to other organizations as well. "You can never say no. You just have to divide yourself five different ways and say yes." Could she talk to families at the health department? Yes! Could she help a customer fill out a job application? Yes! Could she translate at the church health fair? Yes! Could she help a child with homework? Yes! Because families were seeing her everywhere, they began to feel comfortable with her and began to feel comfortable coming to the library to find her.

The challenge to all this saying yes, of course, is that Adriana is just one person who has youth services responsibilities in addition to being the sole bilingual staff person at her branch. When asked about this, Adriana is quick to point out the support she has received all along the way from her management and her fellow staff members. As people began coming to the library asking for Adriana, her team could see for themselves the results of all this outreach and understand why it is such an important part of her overall job.

Adriana has learned to adapt her programs to what community members actually want, which doesn't always match what she thinks they want! Her bilingual storytime is a great example of this disconnect. Though bilingual storytime was wonderfully successful at engaging the children when she presented it in kindergarten classrooms and other school events, when she offered it in the library, no one would come. Eventually she developed a relationship with a community agency that provided services to Spanish-speaking moms. This organization brought the moms and children together to the library for a storytime. When Adriana asked the women if they would be interested in a weekly program, the response was emphatically positive. However, they were not interested in a bilingual storytime; they wanted it in Spanish only. "They know that the children will learn English in school," Adriana explains. "They want an opportunity to interact with their children just in Spanish, to help pass on the language and maintain this connection to their heritage." So Adriana responded by launching a monolingual Spanish storytime rather than a bilingual one. That program has been ongoing for several years.

There are many more examples like this of creative, responsive outreach projects that Adriana has launched and lessons she has learned along the way. There is a lot of trial and error, and Adriana embraces her work, understanding that it is an ongoing experiment. When asked why outreach to her community matters, she makes it clear that without outreach, the families she is now regularly serving would have no idea what the library has to offer. "In Mexico and Guatemala, libraries are just buildings full of books. There are no community services. It just isn't something they saw growing up." She emphasizes the importance of having a warm, personal touch when she's working with Spanish-speaking customers. "I would never just stand behind the desk and help someone. I come around the desk, shake their hand, introduce myself, and tell them I'm happy to be there to help them. Parents and children greet me with hugs and besitos (kisses on the cheek). This is the way things are done."

Adriana acknowledges that, in many ways, providing outreach to the Latino community in Boone County has been easier for her than it might be for others because she is from Mexico and does speak Spanish. She praises the bravery and the willingness of librarians who don't have this cultural understanding and language skill on their side. She advises librarians in this position to make connections with others in the community who are serving Spanish speakers. "There are always creative ways to work together to be found; you just have to go out there and look."

BRINGING IT BACK TO BILINGUAL STORYTIME

Libraries and librarians who want to develop a bilingual or Spanish-language storytime program have the best of intentions. They recognize a gap in service in their community and want to do what they can to close it. They want Spanish speakers to feel welcome in their buildings and to have full access to their resources and programs. When librarians think about how to begin their bilingual storytime, they often go right to the nuts and bolts of programming, looking for the best bilingual and Spanish titles, appropriate music, recognizable fingerplays and rhymes, traditional oral stories, and tools that help them share early literacy information in Spanish with parents. These components are critical—there can't be a storytime without them! However, it is important to realize that no matter how great the program is, establishing the foundation of service to the Latino and Spanish-speaking community through outreach is a critical component for setting up the program for success.

If you are a frontline librarian or library staff person charged with developing this program, you probably have a number of other programming responsibilities in addition to desk time, collection development, management, and other tasks. It may feel impossible with the time and resources available to truly take on the giant task of thorough outreach. But the program can't succeed without it—so what can be done?

1. **Start the conversation.** Find out what the organization is currently doing to reach Latinos and Spanish speakers. Share this chapter with supervisors and managers and ask what the organization would be willing to do

differently. Frame the conversation in the context of setting up the program for success.

2. **Train staff.** Excellent customer service to all people, regardless of ethnicity or language skills, must be the norm, not the exception. Make the hiring and retention of bicultural and bilingual staff an institutional priority. Ensure that all staff members who are interacting with customers are warm, approachable, and culturally competent and know the appropriate steps to take to serve someone who speaks a language other than English.

3. **Conduct community leader interviews.** Even if there is time for only one interview right now, that's still a place to start. Begin with someone who seems likely to have good information about and relationships with the families the library hopes to serve with its bilingual storytime. Reach out using a personal touch, not just e-mail.

4. **Consider the setting.** Is the library the best place to launch this new program? Could the library use this program as a tool to embed itself in a location that the targeted community already frequents and where community members feel comfortable?

5. **Explore new channels of promotion.** There is nothing wrong with using the library website and flyers to promote the program, but this approach won't be enough on its own. Spanish-language media outlets, networking groups, social media, and word of mouth are important channels for promoting the library to Latino families.

6. **Set realistic goals and evaluate frequently.** How will the library know that this program is successful? What change or outcome is desired? What signs will the library look for to recognize this change or outcome? These are key questions for the library to ask itself when offering any program and particularly when setting up something new.

CONCLUDING THOUGHTS

Bilingual storytime can be a wonderful and well-attended addition to a library's existing lineup of family programs. However, bilingual storytime is rarely enough by itself to bring into the library Latino and Spanish-speaking families who are not already library users. By investing time in strategic outreach to the Latino community, the library can develop new relationships that allow it to be perceived as a trusted and valuable community resource. In addition to supporting the bilingual storytime, such outreach allows the library to better know how to truly make a difference in the lives of more people in its community.

Outreach is not the work of just one person, or even one department. It is an institutional effort, and the value of extending equitable access to all must permeate across all job titles and levels of responsibility. As one of our bilingual storytime contributors, librarian Kelly Von Zee, puts it, "Outreach is my eight-hour-a-day job. Whether I am providing customer service on the desk, presenting bilingual storytime, or being present in the community, the attitude that everyone is welcome and encouraged to be here must be expressed. Nothing happens in a bubble."[5]

NOTES

1. WebJunction, "Spanish Language Outreach Program," www.webjunction.org/explore-topics/slo.html.

2. Yolanda Cuesta, "Community Leader Interview Guide," WebJunction (March 21, 2012), www.webjunction.org/materials/webjunction/Community_Leader_Interview_Guide.html.

3. Personal communication with author (March 2015).

4. Edward Flores and Harry Pachon, "Latinos and Public Library Perceptions," Tomás Rivera Policy Institute and WebJunction (September 2008), www.webjunction.org/content/dam/WebJunction/Documents/webJunction/213544usb_wj_latinos_and_public_library_perceptions.pdf.

5. Personal communication with author (July 2015).

Chapter Three

Bilingual Storytime When You Do Not Speak Spanish

any librarians who are not bilingual are interested in learning how to present bilingual storytime. Let's address this challenge head-on: storytime presenters[1] who do not speak Spanish cannot offer a truly bilingual storytime program on their own. The same is true for presenters who speak Spanish and not English. To present a bilingual storytime on your own, you must be at least conversant in both languages being used in the program. There is a very simple reason for this: presenters leading bilingual storytimes are representing themselves as bilingual and must be able to respond to the needs of the families in attendance regardless of which of the two languages those families prefer to use. It may be possible to select simple books and songs and to practice enough in advance to be able to present an engaging storytime in two languages without conversational skills in both languages. However, what is the value of this if, when a parent asks a question about selecting books for his or her child at the end of the program, the presenter is unable to understand or respond?

At *minimum,* we recommend that anyone offering a bilingual storytime on his or her own be competent enough in both languages to handle basic polite conversation and common library transactions. There are varying levels of language fluency for any language learner. For the purposes of presenting a high-quality bilingual storytime, it may not be necessary to have the highest level of fluency across all subject matter, but being able to communicate with ease is essential. Those presenters who are native Spanish speakers, or who have spent extensive time living in areas of the world where Spanish is spoken, have the advantage of understanding the nuances, wordplay, and subtle meanings of the language that can only come with time and experience. However, not having Spanish-language skills should not deter anyone from designing English-language programming that is inclusive of diverse Latino cultures or offering a bilingual storytime in cooperation with a bilingual partner.

INTENTIONAL INCLUSION OF LATINO CULTURES AND THE SPANISH LANGUAGE IN ENGLISH STORYTIME

Today, many children's librarians are aware that picture books can serve as mirrors (reflecting one's own culture and life experience) and windows (providing a glimpse into other cultures and ways of life).[2] Exposure to positive representations of people from their cultural group is important for children in terms of the development of their ethnic identity and sense of self.[3] In addition, it is valuable for children of all ethnic groups to see positive representations of people from other cultures. With some self-awareness and intentionality, storytime presenters can ensure that their English-language storytime programs are inclusive of and positively portray diverse Latino cultures.

The most obvious way to be inclusive of Latinos in English-language storytime is to use books created by Latino authors and illustrators. Though we know the number of books published by and about Latinos is still shockingly low (only about 125 of the approximately five thousand children's books published in 2014),[4] we also know that excellent books by talented authors and illustrators are being published. Many of these books are written in English and sprinkled with a few Spanish words and phrases. Quite often, books written in this style include a glossary or pronunciation guide, or both, to aid readers who may not already be familiar with the Spanish vocabulary. Readers can also use an online dictionary that provides audio support (such as www.wordreference.com) to hear the word pronounced. Audio assistance along with a little practice should make these books quite easy to read and enjoy. Although many excellent books are written employing this technique, others are of less quality. Be critical when evaluating books written in this style, particularly if they are written by non-Latino authors. Specifically, watch out for books that make up Spanish words (as in the *Skippyjon Jones* books by Judy Schachner) by using techniques such as adding an -*o* to the end of an English word in order to make it seem more Latin. This practice trivializes the Spanish language and can be very offensive. Also, some books that use this technique incorporate Spanish words in an odd or awkward manner that does little to enhance the story or make the story more authentic and instead simply seem to be an afterthought or a publishing gimmick. For a list of high-quality books with Latino content that are recommended for English-language storytime, see chapter 7.

Non-bilingual presenters can also use bilingual books. It is common that non-bilingual librarians and presenters are hesitant to use bilingual books in their English-language storytime programs. The assumption is often that one must be able to read these books in both languages in order to use them. However, bilingual books are written entirely in English in addition to the other language, and there is absolutely no reason not to use them in storytime. In fact, not using these books in programming contributes to a real problem in terms of the diversity of library collections. Many picture books by and about Latinos are published bilingually in order to extend their reach and widen their audience. However, in libraries, bilingual books are often cataloged as foreign language books. Then they are placed in the foreign language section, the quality and discoverability of which varies from library to library. In some libraries this area may be easy to locate; in others, it is tucked away somewhere that is not obvious and is difficult to find, particularly for people who may be new to the library or have limited English skills. Either way, by placing the bilingual books in the foreign language section, librarians greatly diminish the likelihood that English-only parents will discover the books and check them out. If the books are not easily discoverable, their circulation numbers suffer. For most libraries, circulation numbers are the guiding data that drive decisions when weeding. So, through no fault of their own, bilingual books are often doomed from the start to be checked out less and weeded more. Pulling these books out of the foreign language section and including them in programs such as storytime and in the displays in the children's area can help them to be more discoverable by the families who can enjoy them. In addition, the use of bilingual books in storytimes demonstrates that the library has materials available in other languages. Figure 3.1 offers suggested guidelines for evaluating and selecting high-quality bilingual books.

Another way to be inclusive of Latino cultures is to tell traditional stories and folktales from the Latino world. Folktales and oral storytelling are important in many cultures, including Latino cultures. Folktales are often how families pass down morals, social expectations, and behavioral guidelines. Storytelling is also a cultural art form. There is a great wealth of traditional Latino stories that are fun to share in storytime. In addition to oral storytelling, presenters can use a variety of techniques to share traditional stories, including draw-and-tell, creative dramatics, the use of props, puppetry, and the use of a flannelboard.

Non-bilingual presenters can make efforts to include the Spanish language in storytime by using bilingual or Spanish music and songs. Spanish children's music can easily be incorporated when playing or dancing with props such as a parachute, egg shakers, colored scarves, or musical instruments. Try dancing along to bilingual movement songs or sharing very simple Spanish rhymes, such as the traditional "Chocolate" or "Cabeza, hombros, rodillas, pies," a Spanish-language version of "Head, Shoulders, Knees, and Toes."

Finally, non-bilingual presenters can use many existing resources to communicate school readiness and early literacy messages to Spanish-speaking parents, including encouraging parents to interact with children in the language that they know best. One such resource is ¡Colorín Colorado! (www.colorincolorado .org). This bilingual website is a treasure trove of resources for librarians, teachers, and families of English language learners. Dozens of parent-friendly articles about early literacy and school readiness are available on the website and can be printed in both English and Spanish. The site also has Reading Tip Sheets available in eleven languages for parents of children of various ages.

FIGURE 3.1

EVALUATING AND SELECTING BILINGUAL AND CULTURALLY RELEVANT BOOKS

When selecting specific bilingual titles to use in storytimes and library collections, librarians might find the following guidelines useful.

- **Placement of the Spanish version of the narrative.** Does English text take precedence over Spanish text in the physical layout of the book? For instance, in many bilingual books the English version of the narrative always precedes the Spanish version and is printed either above or to the left of the Spanish. Placement of English before Spanish suggests that English is considered the more important language.

- **Methods for distinguishing between the Spanish and English texts.** Consider how the English and Spanish versions of the text are differentiated from one another. Are different colors, formatting, or symbols used to distinguish the two languages? Is it easy for emergent readers to know which text is the English and which is the Spanish?

- **Color and formatting (size and weight of type) of the Spanish text.** In numerous bilingual children's books, the Spanish version of the text is printed in an illegible font, in italics, or in a color (such as light blue) that is difficult to read when placed on the page background. When the English version of a text can be clearly read and the Spanish version cannot, it further communicates to readers that the English narrative takes precedence.

- **Spelling, grammar, and punctuation of Spanish text.** Assess the Spanish version of the text. Are words spelled correctly? Are grammar and punctuation, such as diacritics, used appropriately? Depending on the publisher of the bilingual book, the Spanish translation might not be edited at all or might be edited by someone with only a cursory understanding of Spanish.

- **Version of Spanish used.** Spanish, like English and other languages, includes formal, regional, dialectical, and universal neutral versions. It is important that the Spanish used in a book mirrors, or at least does not conflict with, the specific Latino culture being represented. For instance, a book about a Puerto Rican family might use regional or dialectical elements of Spanish spoken in Puerto Rico or among the Puerto Rican culture. It would be a mistake to use Mexican Spanish in this particular book to represent the language of the Puerto Rican characters. On the other hand, a book might be culturally generic, and universal neutral Spanish would be more appropriate than formal or regional Spanish.

- **Accuracy of translations.** Literal translations can lose cultural nuances and result in stilted language. Many words in Spanish do not have an English equivalent. A proper translation will reflect the general idea of a text while remaining true to the author's intent. It is especially important for rhymes and poems to be rewritten when translated to maintain the pacing and flow of the original language.

❯ For more information on selecting bilingual books, consult articles and books written by the late Isabel Schon, a dynamic advocate for authentic Spanish and bilingual books for children. A useful examination of how publishers determine the Spanish version of a text can be found in the article "Descubriendo el sabor: Spanish Bilingual Book Publishing and Cultural Authenticity."[1]

Useful sources for locating culturally relevant children's books are the three major awards for Latino children's literature.

- **Pura Belpré Award.** Given each year by the Association for Library Service to Children and REFORMA (The National Association to Promote Library and Information Services to Latinos and the Spanish-Speaking), this award recognizes Latino authors and illustrators for the publication of children's books that authentically and accurately portray Latino cultural experiences (see www.ala.org/alsc/belpre).

- **Tomás Rivera Mexican American Children's Book Award.** Established by the Texas State University College of Education, this literary prize is given to children's book authors and illustrators whose work celebrates the lives and experiences of Mexican Americans in the United States (see http://riverabookaward.org/).

- **Américas Award.** Sponsored by the Consortium of Latin American Studies Programs (CLASP), this award honors and commends authors and illustrators who create high-quality children's and young adult books that represent Latin American, Caribbean, or Latino cultures (see http://claspprograms.org/americasaward).

NOTE
1. Jamie Campbell Naidoo and Julia López-Robertson, "Descubriendo el sabor: Spanish Bilingual Book Publishing and Cultural Authenticity," *Multicultural Review* 16, no. 4 (2007): 24–37.

Another excellent resource is the Para los Niños family literacy program (www.cmhouston.org/para-los-ninos) developed by the Children's Museum of Houston and the Houston Public Library. This program, which has been presented by libraries in numerous states, uses books and activities to help parents in their efforts to raise school-ready kids. The entire curriculum, including parent instructions for all activities and crafts, is freely available online in both English and Spanish. Non-bilingual presenters can easily use these materials to incorporate the activities into their storytimes (for example, by setting up parent-led crafts or discovery centers to work on after the program), providing the instructions and benefits of the activity in both English and Spanish. For additional recommended Spanish and bilingual resources that help promote early literacy and school readiness, see chapter 7. A summary of recommended best practices for including Latino cultures and the Spanish language when presenting English-language storytime can be found in figure 3.2.

FIGURE 3.2

BEST PRACTICES FOR INCLUDING LATINO CULTURES AND THE SPANISH LANGUAGE IN ENGLISH STORYTIME

1	Intentionally include high-quality children's literature by and about Latinos.
2	Critically evaluate English-language picture books that include Spanish words for authenticity, particularly when written by non-Latino authors.
3	Use bilingual books; it's okay to read them in English only!
4	Use folktales from the Spanish-speaking world for storytelling, flannelboards, puppetry, and the like.
5	Incorporate Spanish-language and bilingual children's music and rhymes.

WORKING WITH A BILINGUAL PARTNER

The second strategy that a non-bilingual presenter can use to present bilingual storytime is to work with a partner who is bilingual. This arrangement can have many variations, but ideally each person involved brings valuable skills to the table, resulting in a true partnership. Generally, the library presenter brings skills in designing and implementing developmentally appropriate storytime programs. This ability includes knowledge of diverse children's literature, the mechanics of storytime, how to engage children of various ages, and how to deliver relevant early literacy messages to parents and caregivers. The partner brings language skills and, ideally, cultural knowledge and community connections. A summary of recommended best practices when working with a partner to present bilingual storytime can be found in figure 3.3.

Whom the presenter selects for a partner and how this person is identified will vary from community to community. This section presents basic ideas of how to begin the search, but ultimately the result will depend on the relationships that exist within the community. Ideally, your partner will be someone from within, or with strong connections to, the local Latino community and will be well compensated for his or her time. Depending on the availability of the partner(s), tandem bilingual programming may work best as a periodic event (i.e., monthly or quarterly) rather than as an ongoing, weekly offering.

FIGURE 3.3	
BEST PRACTICES FOR PRESENTING BILINGUAL STORYTIME WITH A PARTNER	
1	Look for a bilingual storytime partner from within, or with strong connections to, the local Latino community that you are trying to reach. Preferably the partner will be from an organization with goals similar to those of the library.
2	Provide plenty of time to offer any needed storytime training to your partner and to practice your programs together before presenting them.
3	Start your program slowly, perhaps offering a one-time pilot program rather than launching right into an ongoing weekly program, to ensure the partnership is the right fit.
4	Have a backup plan for your program in case something happens to prevent your partner from attending.
5	Celebrate your partner's skills, talents, and dedication; be sure your partner knows she or he is appreciated.

Library Staff

Some libraries may have a bilingual staff person who works in another department (not children's services) with whom you can partner to offer a bilingual storytime. This person may or may not have experience working with children. If possible, gain supervisor approval and then approach the person about this opportunity in a positive way. Adding a new responsibility to someone's work life always goes best if he or she sees the value in the change and agrees to it voluntarily, rather than having it mandated externally. Share the intention of the program and what the partner's role would be in helping to bring that goal to life. Supervisors should ensure that the bilingual staff person's responsibilities are appropriately modified to accommodate this new role and that the presenter has plenty of time not only to design the program but also to provide training to the bilingual partner and to practice the program in advance. Rapport and energy between the two program leaders is essential for tandem programming to be enjoyable for all. It is crucial to provide adequate time for the partners to establish this relationship, particularly in the beginning.

Community Agency Employees

Another option is to work with a bilingual partner from a community agency whose mission is similar to that of the library—for example, a Head Start teacher or a Family Resource Center coordinator. The outreach work the library is already doing (see chapter 2) will be of great value when identifying people in the community who might be a good fit. Meet with any potential partners at their convenience to present this partnership opportunity. Ideally, the program would align so well with the goals of a potential partner's organization that the person would be able to participate as part of the regular workday, ensuring appropriate compensation. Inquire about the potential partner's experience in working with children and explain some of the principles or standards used in designing library storytime. If the partner has experience working with young children and families, she or he may be able to help in the program planning in addition to presentation. Work together to find a fair balance of responsibilities between the organizations, not only in terms of developing the program but also in deciding where it will be held, how it will be promoted, and so on. Because the needs of two organizations will need to be balanced in this approach, more planning time may be needed on the front end before the program can be launched. However, the result can be a thriving partnership that brings the resources and the passion of two organizations together, resulting in improved service to the targeted community, as well as other partnership opportunities unforeseen at the outset of the relationship.

Volunteers

For some libraries, working with volunteers may be the best approach, though admittedly it can be challenging. The best case scenario for working with volunteers to present bilingual storytime is to have a relationship with a Latino civic organization that is seeking volunteer opportunities for its membership. This might be a professional organization, a community organization, or a student organization. In this scenario, interested members with the necessary language skills could attend a training presented by the library that introduces members to fundamentals of storytime and their role as a bilingual copresenter. The design of the storytime program would be mostly left to the library presenter, although this approach may change over time as the volunteers get a feel for how to design and present a storytime. It may be helpful to designate one or two volunteers as materials selectors who could help advise you on the quality of translations, the familiarity of traditional songs, and the like. The library presenter could schedule the volunteers on a rotating basis to copresent the bilingual storytime. The potential disadvantage to this approach is that the presenter would be working with several different volunteers, which can be challenging in terms of management and the establishment of a programming style. However, by engaging an active Latino organization, you will likely achieve more community buy-in for your program.

When working with an established organization is not an option, consider approaching a bilingual community member whom you know personally. Being dependent on one volunteer puts the library at the mercy of that person's schedule, however. A weekly, ongoing storytime may not be an option. There is also an ethical challenge to consider—is it appropriate to depend on an unpaid community volunteer to provide service to the Spanish-speaking members of the community?

Students Learning Spanish

Finally, some libraries may consider reaching out to local high school or college students who are learning Spanish. Although this approach could help students to gain needed volunteer experience and help build a relationship between the library and the school or college, the library presenter should think critically about, and talk openly with the students' instructor to determine, whether the language skills of the students meet the standard previously discussed for bilingual storytime. In this scenario, the library presenter will carry the majority of the responsibility for designing the program and will need to provide basic storytime training to the students.

In figure 3.4 one library assistant recounts her experiences working with bilingual partners and offers suggestions for success.

CONCLUDING THOUGHTS

Determining who can present a bilingual storytime can be a tricky matter. A number of factors influence this issue, including library resources, community diversity, and even geographical location. In the ideal scenario, a library has many bilingual staff members at all levels of professional responsibility who reflect the diversity of the community served. However, this ideal does not yet match the reality of library staffing in many places. Communities speaking languages other than English should not have to wait for libraries to fully actualize into their ideal versions before having access to important services and programs, such as storytime. But language skills and cultural competence are critically important when evaluating who is and who is not qualified to present bilingual storytime.

Bilingual storytime presenters must be *at least* conversationally fluent in both languages being used in order to present the program on their own. Although not everyone is qualified to present bilingual storytime alone, anyone leading storytime can take simple steps to ensure that the programs include and positively portray diverse Latino cultures and the Spanish language. Non-bilingual presenters who want to offer a truly bilingual storytime have a variety of options for finding a bilingual partner who can help in this endeavor. This chapter has presented several potential strategies for finding such a partner; the best fit for any one organization will depend on the resources and relationships in the local community.

Although it takes time to find the right fit, programming in tandem with a community partner can be great fun. There is no way to know what hidden talents or wonderful skills your partner will bring to the table without providing opportunities to try lots of things; experimentation is encouraged! Two

FIGURE 3.4

CASE STUDY | WORKING WITH BILINGUAL PARTNERS

Christian Reynolds, a library assistant at the Alexandria (Virginia) Public Library, does not speak much Spanish, but she is eager to serve the growing Latino and Spanish-speaking community. The following is a synopsis of an interview with Christian about a specific program she recently offered and what she learned along the way.

Q	**Describe your outreach efforts to Spanish speakers in your community.**
A	The outreach activity that I do most often is to visit a local health clinic that serves a large number of Spanish-speaking families. I always go with a Spanish-speaking partner. In the past this has at times been other staff, but currently I'm visiting with a volunteer who is Latina and bilingual. While families are in the waiting room, I read books with the children and my partner speaks with the adults about the library and its services and explains how to obtain a card. This outreach has been successful at spreading the word about the library and building trust.
Q	**You recently decided to present a bilingual storytime, though you are not bilingual yourself. Can you describe this process?**
A	Though our outreach work has been helpful for making initial contact, we still felt like we had work to do in terms of welcoming Latino families into the library itself. This prompted the idea of a grand scale bilingual storytime. We wanted it to be in the library, so we could use the opportunity to introduce the multitude of library resources that are available outside of children's programming, such as our ESL [English as a second language] classes. I worked with two bilingual partners, both of whom are Latina and have experience working with children, to plan and present the program. We held it during evening hours and included food, music, and crafts in addition to stories.
Q	**How did you find your partners?**
A	I actually got quite lucky in finding my partners! Both are library users who had attended programs at the library. The first person I partnered with actually approached the library on her own looking for volunteer opportunities. She had brought her own child to library programs and wanted to help the library specifically with providing programs in Spanish. She is a Spanish teacher. The second partner I found through my volunteer who helps me with my outreach at the health clinic. She is a music teacher.
Q	**Describe the planning process and what it was like working with your partners.**
A	This was a collaborative effort! Each person was able to contribute her own unique skills. One interesting suggestion that came from the volunteers was to move away from the "storytime" name, a term not widely recognized in the community being targeted, and calling the program instead a "Family Fiesta / Fiesta familiar." My partners were also extremely helpful in promoting the program among Latino and Spanish-speaking families who are not regular library users. Because they are from the community themselves, they had the access to promote the program via word of mouth to many more people than I would have been able to reach on my own.
Q	**So . . . how did it go?**
A	It was great! People began arriving early, so we spent time making maraca crafts and one of our volunteers did face painting while people were coming in. Then we got started with live music before sharing a few stories and a meal. We provided an extensive spread of food, including empanadas and chips and dip. More than thirty children were present, plus their parents. Whole families were enjoying the program together. Though I don't know specifically how many were brand new to the library, I do know that I met a lot of new families. Our intention with this program was to create an environment that clearly said, "You are welcome here!" And in that respect, I think it was a great success. Going forward, we are considering using this model to provide similar programs that are welcoming and inclusive for other culturally and linguistically diverse groups in our community as well.
Q	**Do you have any words of advice to share with other library staff members who may not be bilingual themselves but who want to provide bilingual programming?**
A	I'm not sure that I have a specific piece of generalized advice, but I can speak to a few things that I noticed really worked for us. It helped to have the budget to be able to provide food, and offering the program at night seemed to be a good choice. We asked the people from the Latino community with whom we had already developed relationships to help us spread the word. Just having our Spanish flyer alone wasn't enough; the people who talked with their friends and neighbors made a real difference in terms of bringing people into the library. 📁

presenters working together are often able to bring to life more creative and ambitious storytelling than a single presenter can manage alone. Most important, by working with a bilingual partner, presenters who lack Spanish-language skills themselves are able to make more meaningful connections with Latino and Spanish-speaking families than they would be able to make without such support.

NOTES

1. To include both librarians and other library professionals and paraprofessionals, the term *presenter* will be used throughout this chapter to refer to anyone who may be presenting bilingual storytime programs.
2. Rudine Sims Bishop, "Mirrors, Windows, and Sliding Glass Doors," *Perspectives: Choosing and Using Books for the Classroom* 6, no. 3 (1990): ix–xi.
3. Jamie Campbell Naidoo, "Embracing the Face at the Window: Latino Representation in Children's Literature and the Ethnic Identity Development of Latino Children," in *Celebrating Cuentos: Promoting Latino Children's Literature and Literacy in Classrooms and Libraries*, ed. Jamie Campbell Naidoo (Santa Barbara, CA: Libraries Unlimited, 2011), 19–44.
4. Cooperative Children's Book Center, "Children's Books by and about People of Color and First/Native Nations Published in the United States" (2015), https://ccbc .education.wisc.edu/books/pcstats.asp.

Chapter Four

Bilingual Storytime
One Program, Many Ways

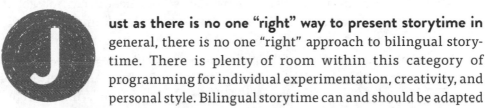

Just as there is no one "right" way to present storytime in general, there is no one "right" approach to bilingual storytime. There is plenty of room within this category of programming for individual experimentation, creativity, and personal style. Bilingual storytime can and should be adapted to best suit community needs. However, just as we have standards and practices that are generally accepted as helpful guidelines for designing successful storytime programs, we can set forth recommended frameworks for bilingual storytime, which is what this chapter intends to do. Most, if not all, of the well-established best practices from general storytime programming will still apply to planning a bilingual storytime. For example, bilingual storytime should be age-appropriate, should incorporate a variety of materials (not just books), should include materials by and about diverse populations, should model early literacy practices, and should be engaging and fun. This chapter will help you clarify your reasons for establishing a bilingual storytime and will present various approaches for designing it.

IDENTIFYING THE INTENTION

Before jumping into the "how" of bilingual storytime, it is helpful to clarify the "why," because an organization's intention and rationale for establishing such a program will impact how that program is designed. Let's look at a few reasons why you might wish to establish a bilingual storytime and how these types of programs may differ.

New Service for a Growing Latino Immigrant Community

Probably the most common reason why an organization chooses to offer a bilingual storytime is to provide a new service for a growing Latino immigrant community. As we discussed in chapter 2, bilingual storytime is not recommended as a first step for bringing into the library families who are not already library users. In this case, outreach is critical to set up the bilingual storytime for success. However, in conjunction with such outreach, a bilingual storytime can be a wonderful service to offer. Here, the key role of the program is to provide positive, welcoming exposure to the library for a community that may not already be familiar with library services. A program that intends to connect Latino immigrants with library service should be offered at a time and in a location that are convenient for the targeted families to attend. The program may be held off-site rather than in the library and may provide opportunities for families to socialize and ask any library-related questions that they may have. The presenters will be doing much more than just presenting bilingual storytime: they are the face of the organization and will be building relationships with the families being served.

As presenters gain the trust of the families served, they will likely be asked for help with questions in many areas of life (i.e., school, health, law, jobs, etc.). Presenters should be able to provide relevant library-related information and should be well versed in the services available in the community in order to make referrals when questions fall outside the scope of library service. In many ways, when serving a new Latino immigrant community is the intention of the bilingual storytime, the nuts and bolts of the bilingual storytime itself are secondary in importance to the real function of the program, which is to embed the library as a valued and trusted community service.

Early Literacy

In the last decade or so, *early literacy* has become a ubiquitous term in the world of children's librarianship. Helping children to develop a strong foundation in early literacy skills is perhaps the single greatest benefit of storytime programming. Thanks to the framework provided by Every Child Ready to Read, librarians across the country have come to understand *why* we engage with kids in the ways we do in a storytime program, and they are able to quickly and positively communicate those messages to parents in order to empower parents to continue the practices long after the storytime program is over. Supporting young children's early literacy skill development is a wonderful reason to offer a bilingual storytime or a storytime done completely in another language. More discussion on the choice between a monolingual Spanish or a bilingual Spanish-English storytime can be found in figure 4.1. Research makes clear that it is important for parents to engage with children using the language that they know best. By using their home language, parents are able to communicate more sophisticated ideas, use richer language, and more easily play with sounds, all of which help children develop critical early literacy skills. With a strong foundation in early literacy in the home language, children are also able to more easily acquire another language, such as English, when they get to school.[1]

However, take a moment to consider the parents' perspective. Many parents who speak a language other than English at home strongly desire their children to learn English well. Many communities have very few, if any, supports that encourage parents to engage in home language use with their children. It is not hard to understand why, then, it is at times counterintuitive for parents to interact with their children in their home language. Parents may feel pressure to interact in English, even if they are not able to speak it as well as their home language. A bilingual storytime can be a wonderful way to communicate the benefits of interacting in the home language and to show the specific resources that the library has freely available in languages other than English.

FIGURE 4.1

BILINGUAL STORYTIME VERSUS SPANISH-ONLY STORYTIME

"Which is better—bilingual storytime or Spanish-only storytime?" This frequently asked question can be somewhat controversial. Our opinion is that bilingual storytime is not inherently better than Spanish-only storytime, nor vice versa. Each has its benefits and its place.

Benefits of Spanish-Only Storytime

- Monolingual Spanish storytime has the distinct benefit of offering 100 percent immersion in Spanish. This approach clearly demonstrates to parents that interacting with their children in Spanish is valuable, with far-reaching educational and cultural benefits. These programs generally target native Spanish speakers, so attendees might be more comfortable knowing they are with others who share many aspects of their culture and experience. As the stories and books are shared in one language only, it is easier to use longer books that communicate more sophisticated ideas. Monolingual Spanish storytime helps to support sequential bilingualism, in which the home language is developed first and the other language is introduced later.[1] This type of program would be best given by a bilingual presenter, preferably from (or having extensive knowledge of and experience working with) the cultural group most represented in the area.

Benefits of Bilingual Storytime

- Bilingual storytime has the benefit of exposing children and families to both Spanish and English simultaneously. This approach allows for the celebration of bilingualism in a public space. In some parts of the country, there may be few or no other public spaces where this occurs. Because bilingual storytime appeals to different families for different reasons, attendance at these programs is often quite diverse. Such inclusion provides community members, whose lives may otherwise be quite segregated, an opportunity to interact and even learn a little about other cultures. For bilingual families raising bilingual children, this type of program helps to support simultaneous bilingualism.[2] For children whose home language is Spanish, this exposure to English can help ease the transition to the full English immersion they will experience when they begin school. Bilingual storytime can be presented by a single bilingual presenter or by a pair of presenters working in tandem.

❯ Whether an organization decides to offer a Spanish-only program, a bilingual program, or some combination of the two should not be based on an interpretation of what the library world presumes is "right." Rather, the decision should reflect the community's values and needs as well as the resources (including human) the organization has available to dedicate to the program. Those offering Spanish-only storytime and those offering bilingual storytime ultimately have much more in common than they have separating them. Both camps want to see Latino families included in and actively engaged with the library; they want to see all children start school with a strong foundation in early literacy skills; and they both want to celebrate the beauty of cultural heritage and the rich diversity of their communities.

NOTES

1. Gilda Martinez, "Bilingual Language Development," in *Early Literacy Programming en Español: Mother Goose on the Loose® Programs for Bilingual Learners*, by Betsy Diamant-Cohen (New York: Neal-Schuman, 2010), 11.
2. Ibid., 13.

An early literacy focused storytime is about empowerment. Parents should be encouraged to participate actively and be praised for their efforts. Parents should leave the program feeling confident that they have the tools and the skills to help their children develop the early literacy skills they need. Most important, parents should understand the value of what they have to offer as their child's first teacher by interacting in the language they know best. Multiple approaches and frameworks would work for a bilingual storytime that intends to promote early literacy practices. The keys are that early literacy practices are modeled throughout, early literacy messages are communicated to parents in both of the languages represented, and parents are encouraged to continue the practices in the language they know best.

Language Learning

If the goal of the bilingual storytime is to teach children a new language (i.e., to teach Spanish to English-speaking children or to teach English to Spanish-speaking children), then the storytime is going to be highly structured and grounded in the research and best practices coming from the education world, particularly the realm of serving dual language learners (DLLs) in early childhood settings. Materials may be used differently in a program designed to support language learning as opposed to another intention. For example, if language learning is the goal, it may not be best to read bilingual books in both English and Spanish simultaneously. Rather, it may be better to read a bilingual book through completely in the home language first, and later read the book again in the second language, emphasizing key words and actions. This strategy allows the children to focus on one language at a time.[2] Repetition and opportunities for hands-on learning and individual conversations are also highly recommended strategies when language learning is the goal. This type of programming is probably best suited for a presenter with an education background, particularly one with experience working with DLLs. Organizations offering this type of programming may want to set it up as a series with advanced registration, so that a consistent group is being served and the learning can progressively build from program to program throughout the series.

Celebrating Bilingualism

Bilingual storytime provides an opportunity to celebrate bilingualism through language exposure. Bilingualism brings many benefits, including the obvious one of enabling communication with more people. Research also indicates that bilingual individuals are more creative and have greater earning power over the course of their lives than monolingual people.[3] For many, bilingualism is also an important part of cultural heritage. A storytime program that celebrates bilingualism should include diverse materials, not only using books by and about people of diverse cultures but also incorporating a variety of techniques, such as storytelling, songs, and games. The presenters should ensure that the atmosphere is welcoming and that all families feel included.

Of course, many bilingual storytime programs will be designed to respond to a combination of these intentions, and that is fine. A bilingual storytime primarily focused on bringing library service to a new community can still make a positive impact on the early literacy skill development of the children being served. The point of this section is not to suggest that bilingual storytime should have just one goal. Rather, the purpose is to help your organization think through its primary reason for choosing to establish this program in order to more clearly understand what resources the library must be prepared to commit and how to appropriately evaluate the program for success.

BILINGUAL STORYTIME FRAMEWORKS

There are many ways to structure a bilingual storytime. The presenter's intention for the program, the resources available, and the presenter's personal storytime style will all influence the program design. Presenters may choose to stick with one framework consistently or to experiment with several approaches from session to session. This section will explore two common approaches to bilingual storytime: using Spanish and English simultaneously and using them separately.

Rather than suggesting that one way is better or right, we encourage presenters to experiment and to be responsive to what works best for their specific community. The more experience you gain with bilingual storytime programming, the more comfortable you will become, eventually finding an approach that is uniquely your own.

Using English and Spanish Simultaneously

In this approach, materials are shared in both Spanish and English at the same time. For example, when reading a book, one section or page may be read first in Spanish and then in English (or vice versa) until the entire book has been read in this manner. Storytelling is done in a similar way. Songs and rhymes are shared in English and Spanish as well, though this technique can be trickier because of the difficulty in preserving both meaning and rhyme across translations. Therefore, it may be more convenient to choose bilingual songs or to alternate between delivering a song or rhyme completely in Spanish and then in English (or vice versa).

Be sure to honor a child's attention span when selecting materials for this style of program. Brief books (one to three lines of text per page) generally work best for young children. Trying to read a lengthy picture book in two languages can be the kiss of death for bilingual storytime, as younger children may lose interest. Longer books may be more appropriate for classroom visits to elementary students in dual language education programs. Depending on length, bilingual books and translated books can both be used, but when using translations, we recommend having both versions of the book available in the collection rather than translating books yourself. More information on this topic can be found in figure 4.2.

When program partners are working in tandem (as described in the previous chapter), each presenter should hold a copy of the book (either bilingual or in the language the presenter is using). Bilingual presenters offering a bilingual storytime on their own may choose which language of a translated book to hold during storytime (i.e., the Spanish version or the English version). When reading a monolingual book in a bilingual style, we recommend holding the Spanish version of the book as this clearly demonstrates to the audience that the library has picture books available for checkout in Spanish. Presenters using this approach may find it helpful (particularly for books written in rhyme) to have the text of the version they are not reading (i.e., the text of the English version if the book being used is in Spanish) typed and taped to the back of the book to

FIGURE 4.2

TRANSLATING MATERIALS ON THE FLY

A method sometimes used by bilingual storytime presenters, particularly when they lack high-quality and age-appropriate picture books in Spanish in their collections, is to translate materials on the fly, meaning that the presenter translates monolingual English books into Spanish. Though there is nothing inherently wrong with this approach, here are a few things to consider:

1	**This approach does not demonstrate that the library has children's materials available in Spanish.** Remember, depending on who your audience is, you cannot assume that all program attendees (particularly in an outreach program in a venue outside the library) know that the library has Spanish-language children's books available. By using Spanish and bilingual books in your storytime, you are showing (rather than telling) what the library has to offer.
2	**This approach does not model the use of books that monolingual Spanish-speaking parents can feel empowered to use at home with their children.** One of the greatest benefits of a storytime program is to model early literacy practices, particularly encouraging parents to continue the practices at home in the language that they know best. When monolingual Spanish-speaking parents see materials written only in English in storytime, they may feel discouraged rather than empowered.
3	**This approach does not invest in the development of a high-quality Spanish and bilingual collection.** Libraries have a responsibility to develop collections that meet the needs of the communities they serve, including providing materials in other languages. Bilingual storytime presenters have an opportunity to advocate for having excellent materials available not only for storytime but for families to check out and use in their home language as well.
4	**This approach relies on the use of popular English-language books rather than the use of books originally written bilingually or in Spanish.** Diversity matters—period. As librarians, we have a responsibility to ensure that diverse voices, including those of Latino authors and illustrators who may be creating bilingual and Spanish-language materials, are included in our programs.

refer to as needed. This way the presenter does not have to memorize the exact text as written.

Kelly Von Zee provides a bilingual storytime that uses English and Spanish simultaneously at the Addison (Illinois) Public Library. Her program is for children from birth to age 5 but is generally designed for the toddler crowd. She uses lots of fingerplays and rhymes, mixes in one book during each program, and includes key messages about early literacy practices for parents in both English and Spanish. She uses PowerPoint to share the words to the songs and rhymes in both English and Spanish, so that parents who speak either language can understand what is being said. Sometimes songs and rhymes are shared in one language only, because there is no adequate translation to the other language.

Kelly says that her favorite part of her bilingual storytime is the interaction that takes place among the families who attend, despite their language barriers. The Addison Public Library serves a very diverse community, with many community members speaking languages other than English at home, including Spanish and Polish. However, even though the community is diverse, there are few opportunities for people from different cultures to mingle. Providing this opportunity for multicultural interaction is one of the advantages of the bilingual storytime program. Kelly's bilingual storytime also gives adults an opportunity to begin or continue their language learning and provides an opportunity to model bilingualism as a positive attribute. She admits that bilingual storytime can be tricky and that it would be easier for her as a staff person to plan a monolingual program, but the positive benefits she sees the program bringing to her community make it worth the extra effort. Examples of Kelly's bilingual storytimes are presented in chapter 6.

Using English and Spanish Separately

Another approach to bilingual storytime is to present the program using both English and Spanish materials but using them separately, rather than providing direct translation. Depending on the age of the children, presenters may be able to use slightly longer books and stories with this approach because the materials are being shared in only one language at a time. When using this approach, presenters may choose to replace songs and rhymes used in one language with similarly themed songs and rhymes in the other language rather than using translations, unless the translations are very high quality and the rhymes and songs are equally fun and engaging in both languages.

Several variations are possible for a program that uses English and Spanish separately. For example, you may choose to select a theme and use totally different books, songs, and rhymes in each language on that theme. Or you may choose to use the same materials (i.e., bilingual books) first in one language and then in the other. Another method is to share the first half of the program completely in one language and then present the second half of the program in the other language. Clearly, this approach provides ample room for experimentation.

Using Spanish and English separately aligns with strategies recommended for teachers working with dual language learners in the classroom and may be the most appropriate approach for programs designed for language learning.[4] The home language can be used first to activate the children's background knowledge, then the second language can be introduced, emphasizing key words and phrases. This approach can be wonderful for bilingual families because it provides an opportunity for immersive interaction in each language. However, if you are working with a group that is not bilingual already, you risk losing the children's attention when engaging for a long time in a language some of them may not know well. A similar risk is that non-bilingual parents may feel alienated or disengaged when the interaction is taking place solely in the language they don't know well.

Maria Lee Goodrich, of the Novato Library of the Marin County (California) Free Library, provides bilingual storytime to three preschool classes in her library's service area. Maria Lee uses English and Spanish materials separately without direct translation. For classes with the youngest children, the storytime is very active, with lots of movement songs and activities. For classes with older children, there is more dialogue about the information shared in the program and the books. She typically reads one Spanish book and one English book (a separate title, not a translation) per program, while also mixing in songs and rhymes. Maria Lee does point out key words in English as she reads a Spanish book (and vice versa) to support vocabulary development. She often incorporates American Sign Language into her programs as well, making them a trilingual experience!

Maria Lee's former experience as an immersion teacher informs her approach and her understanding of the value of providing students a truly immersive experience in two languages. Because her storytime is in a classroom setting, she is working with the same children throughout the year. She is able to watch the students develop new language skills in both Spanish and English over time. For her, this opportunity to help cultivate bilingualism among the youngest members of her community is what the program is all about.

BILINGUAL STORYTIME FOR VARIOUS AGES

The structure of bilingual storytime should be engaging and appropriate for the ages of the children being targeted. This section will comment briefly on different program approaches appropriate for babies, toddlers, preschoolers, and mixed-age crowds. A sample template for planning a program for each of these age groups is also provided. Suggested best practices for bilingual storytime are summarized in figure 4.3.

FIGURE 4.3

BEST PRACTICES FOR BILINGUAL STORYTIME

1	Set up your program for success with strong, ongoing outreach efforts.
2	Offer your program at a time and in a location that are convenient for the families you want to reach, even if this means presenting your program outside the library.
3	Use books created by Latino authors and illustrators from a variety of cultures and countries.
4	Use engaging books and other materials that represent non-Latino cultures as well, including indigenous cultures and people of color.
5	When using translated books, be sure to assess the quality of the translation. Look for translators who have a vast body of work and who are well known for delivering high-quality content.
6	Use songs, rhymes, fingerplays, and games traditional to various Latino cultures, particularly the cultural group(s) that your program is predominantly serving.
7	Use books, songs, and stories that you enjoy. Don't use materials that you don't like; children will feel your hesitation.
8	Look outside the library world to parenting blogs and websites dedicated to multilingual and multicultural families to stay aware of children's music, books, websites, and apps that may be relevant to the families you are serving.
9	Empower parents to engage in early literacy practices at home with their children using the language that they know best. Provide these messages in both English and Spanish.
10	Experiment with a variety of styles of bilingual storytime until you find the one that best suits you and your community. There is no one right way to offer bilingual storytime, so embrace your creativity!

Babies

A program for babies will focus on providing lots of opportunities for loving interaction between the child and the adult caregiver(s). A baby's brain is growing rapidly; exposure to language through songs, rhymes, and books is a great way to help a baby learn about her world and develop the beginnings of language skills.[5] It is important to honor a baby's minimal attention span and keep the program brief. Twenty minutes is generally a good amount of time for this age. The program will consist mostly of rhymes and music, which may be repeated from week to week in order to establish a consistent routine and to help both the babies and the adults learn the material. Incorporate one or two books with minimal text during the program. Bilingual books that present first concepts (such as colors, numbers, and shapes) are excellent choices for a baby storytime. It may be helpful to have a special collection of bilingual board books on hand as part of this program to pass out to caregivers to encourage one-on-one reading with their child. Special time for dancing or free play with age-appropriate manipulatives (i.e., soft toys, bubbles, or balls) may become a much-loved part of your program. Be sure to incorporate early literacy messages to parents in both

FIGURE 4.4

BILINGUAL EARLY LITERACY MESSAGES FOR PARENTS

Early literacy	La alfabetización temprana
Singing, reading, writing, talking, playing	Cantando, leyendo, escribiendo, hablando, jugando
Early literacy is what children know about reading and writing before they know how to read and write.	La alfabetización temprana es lo que los niños saben sobre lectura y escritura antes de que puedan leer y escribir.
It is important to speak and read with your child in your native language!	¡Es importante hablar y leer con su niño en su lengua materna!
Children learn new words through picture books, conversations, and games.	Los niños aprenden palabras nuevas a través de libros ilustrados, conversaciones, y juegos.
Talk with your child every day about things and ideas, even before your child is able to speak.	Hable con su niño todos los días sobre cualquier tema, incluso antes de que el niño comience a hablar.
Hearing words that rhyme will help your child learn that words are made up of small sounds.	Al escuchar palabras que riman, su niño aprende que las palabras están formadas por pequeños sonidos.
Teach your child the different shapes; this prepares your child to learn the letters.	Enséñele las diferentes formas; esto lo preparará para aprender las letras.
Read with your child every day.	Lea con su niño cada día.
Talk with your child as much as possible.	Hable con su niño lo más posible.
Sing with your child and practice rhymes.	Cante con su niño y practique rimas.
Let your child see you reading often.	Deje que su niño lo vea a usted leyendo con frecuencia.
Make reading special and have fun!	¡Haga de la lectura algo especial y disfrútela!

English and Spanish that present the "why" behind the practices you are modeling. Suggestions for early literacy messages for parents are shown in figure 4.4.

Either of the previously described frameworks is appropriate for your bilingual storytime for babies. One option is to present a rhyme or song in one language, followed by a version of the same rhyme or song (if a good translation is available) in the other language or a different rhyme in that language on a similar theme. Another option is to present the entire first half of the program in one language and the second half in the other. For those looking for a premade program model to follow,

Early Literacy Programming en Español: Mother Goose on the Loose Programs for Bilingual Learners by Betsy Diamant-Cohen is an excellent resource. It is filled with dozens of high-quality songs and rhymes in both English and Spanish and comes with a CD as well. The following template is suggested for bilingual storytime for babies.

Sample Template: Bilingual Storytime for Babies

- Welcome / Early Literacy Message (Spanish)
- Welcome / Early Literacy Message (English)
- Opening Song—Spanish
- Opening Song—English
- Spanish Rhyme (repeat twice)
- English Rhyme (repeat twice)
- Bilingual Book
- Independent Reading Time for Caregivers and Children with Bilingual Board Books
- Spanish Rhyme (repeat twice)
- English Rhyme (repeat twice)
- Spanish Rhyme (repeat twice)
- English Rhyme (repeat twice)
- Free Play with Music and Manipulatives
- Closing Song—Spanish
- Closing Song—English

Toddlers

Toddlers have more developed language and gross motor skills than babies. They are curious, and they love to move. It is possible to incorporate more reading in programs for this age, but there should still be ample opportunity to move. Interactive songs, rhymes, and fingerplays between stories will keep the group engaged. Attention spans are still short for toddlers, so programs should generally last no more than thirty minutes. It is important to keep some elements consistent from program to program in order to establish a routine that allows children to know what to expect. First concepts are still important to practice with this age. Remind parents of their special role as their child's first teacher, and encourage them to keep the early literacy practices going at home in the language that they know best. The following template is suggested for bilingual storytime for toddlers.

Sample Template: Bilingual Storytime for Toddlers

- Opening Song (English, Spanish, or both)
- Fingerplay (Spanish)
- Fingerplay (English)
- Bilingual Book (Spanish)
- Bilingual Movement Song
- Rhyme (English)
- Rhyme (Spanish)
- Bilingual Book (English)
- Closing Song (English, Spanish, or both)
- Craft or Play Literacy Time

Preschoolers

Storytime for preschool-age children can be a little longer and can incorporate more reading than programs for toddlers and babies. Books with one to three lines of text per page are generally good choices to read aloud bilingually in preschool storytimes. Try incorporating nonfiction books into programs for this age. Flannelboard stories, storytelling that incorporates puppets or props, and creative dramatics that invite participation are also wonderful techniques to incorporate into bilingual preschool storytimes. Talk with caregivers about basic early literacy, math, and science skills that help their children become school ready. Consider providing opportunities for adults and children to experiment with and explore some of these concepts together, such as through the use of discovery center activities. The following template is suggested for bilingual storytime for preschoolers.

Sample Template: Bilingual Storytime for Preschoolers

- Opening Song (English, Spanish, or both)
- Bilingual Book
- Bilingual Movement Song
- Flannelboard / Prop Story
- Interactive Rhyme (Spanish)
- Interactive Rhyme (English)
- Bilingual Book
- Closing Song (English, Spanish, or both)
- Craft or Discovery Center (be sure to provide instructions in both Spanish and English)

Mixed-Age and Family Programs

It is very common for Latino families with children of various ages to attend storytime together. What a wonderful challenge! Yes, it can be a little difficult to design a storytime program that engages 6-year-olds as well as babies, but with some advance planning and flexibility, bilingual storytime for families can be fun and rewarding for presenters and for families.

Begin by focusing on an age group that most of the program will target (e.g., preschoolers). In general, design most of your program to be appropriate for this age. Then mix in modifications that engage children outside this age range as well. For example, a program could be designed to mostly target preschool-age children, but to keep babies engaged, a selection of board books and soft manipulatives or toys could be available in the room for the parents or caregivers to use at their discretion. At the outset of the program, let the adults know that children of different ages will enjoy the program in different ways, and that is okay! Ask for the adults' help in making sure that the program stays enjoyable for all present—for example, by sitting with their toddler to prevent the child from wandering in front of the book or flannelboard. One way to engage multiple ages is to keep the program interactive. Include activities that engage the entire family, such as games or parachute play. When sharing fingerplays or tickle rhymes for babies and toddlers, invite the older children to help the younger children by playing along. Finally, always have a backup plan. Be prepared to modify your program on the fly as needed to best meet the needs of the children in attendance. For example, if your planned program targets preschool-age children but most of the children in attendance are under age 2, much of what you have planned will not be age appropriate. By having many options prepared in advance, you can adapt the program as needed. The following template is suggested for bilingual storytime for families.

Sample Template: Bilingual Storytime for Families

- Opening Song (Spanish, English, or both)
- Bilingual Flannelboard Rhyme
- Bilingual Book
- Movement Song
- Storytelling or Creative Dramatics
- Movement Song
- Bilingual Book
- Closing Song (Spanish, English, or both)
- Discovery Center or Play Literacy Activity (be sure to provide instructions in both Spanish and English)

CONCLUDING THOUGHTS

Bilingual storytimes—the reasons for implementation, the materials selected, and the style of presentation—are every bit as diverse as the families who enjoy them. Librarians considering a bilingual storytime are advised to think through their intentions and their available resources (human, material, and financial) to select an approach that is appropriate and sustainable. However, experimentation should be encouraged; it takes a little trial and error to develop something new.

Storytime is more than an expected library service; it is often a beloved community institution. Generation after generation, children come to the library and age through the various storytime offerings, creating fond memories as they grow into strong readers. With flexibility, creativity, and patience, bilingual storytime can become another cherished offering in this array of fundamental library experiences.

NOTES

1. Association for Library Service to Children and Public Library Association, "Every Child Ready to Read @ your library Toolkit for Spanish-Speaking Communities," 2nd ed. (Chicago: American Library Association, 2014).

2. Karen Nemeth, *Basics of Supporting Dual Language Learners: An Introduction for Educators of Children from Birth through Age 8* (Washington, DC: National Association for the Education of Young Children, 2012), 44.

3. Kendall King and Alison Mackey, *The Bilingual Edge: Why, When and How to Teach Your Child a Second Language* (New York: HarperCollins, 2007).

4. Nemeth, *Basics of Supporting Dual Language Learners.*

5. Kathy MacMillan and Christine Kirker, *Baby Storytime Magic: Active Early Literacy through Bounces, Rhymes, Tickles, and More* (Chicago: ALA Editions, 2014).

Chapter Five

Using Digital Media in Bilingual Storytimes

Librarians can offer bilingual storytimes using a variety of formats and media. An exciting opportunity that many librarians may not have considered is the use of digital media (digital books, digital apps, online educational games, e-books, etc.) in bilingual programming to meet the educational needs of children. Each year more Latino and Spanish-speaking families and their children engage with digital media through smartphones, computers, and tablet technology. The Joan Ganz Cooney Center at Sesame Workshop indicates that the majority of Latino and Spanish-speaking families use digital media regularly for both educational and recreational purposes.[1] However, within this community, rates of adoption and rationale for use vary significantly depending upon such factors as educational attainment, family income, native-born status, and language capacity (English-dominant, Spanish-dominant, or bilingual English-Spanish).[2] In general, families with higher incomes and those who speak English show higher ownership of digital devices as well as higher use of digital media than do Spanish-dominant families who often have limited access to digital technology, particularly computers and tablets.[3] Latino families with children are also more likely to use digital media compared with families without children because many Latino children use their parents' devices for homework, school projects, and other educational activities.[4]

Unfortunately, there is an acknowledged dearth of Spanish-language materials and resources for caregivers on how to select and use educational digital media with their children as well as limited opportunities to see these media modeled appropriately.[5] The public library with a tech-savvy outreach or children's librarian is the opportune place for these families to engage with bilingual digital media and see them modeled purposefully in early literacy activities. And what better place for this to occur than in bilingual storytime! This chapter explores the potential for using digital media with Latino and Spanish-speaking families and children in bilingual storytimes and provides suggestions for successful programs in libraries and other educational settings. We also share resources for identifying quality digital media to use in bilingual storytimes.

DIGITAL MEDIA IN THE LIVES OF LATINO AND SPANISH-SPEAKING CHILDREN

The idea of using digital media in any type of children's library programming, much less bilingual storytimes, causes great consternation for many outreach and children's librarians. Ostensibly, reluctant librarians are worried that digital media will replace cherished books and literacy activities and will open the door for a completely digital library. Without a doubt, children need physical books, but there is considerable opportunity and increasing support for the use of digital media in storytimes as well. In 2015, the Association for Library Service to Children (ALSC) published a white paper emphasizing the importance of digital media in the lives of children to foster digital literacy development. The paper calls for children's librarians to become media mentors who not only recommend high-quality digital apps and e-books to children and families but also use them in library programming.[6] When used purposefully, appropriately, and in moderation, digital apps, digital picture books, and other forms of digital media can play an integral role in supporting the development of all children, including Latino and Spanish-speaking children. The key for media use with these children, according to noted digital media scholar Lisa Guernsey, is to remember the three Cs: content, context, and child.[7] Each of these key concepts is described in detail in the following paragraphs.

Content in selected digital media. When using digital media with bilingual children, it is helpful for librarians to consider the purpose of the content. Are children learning a new skill, reading a story, or creating something? Are these activities developmentally appropriate? Digital media offer considerable flexibility to meet the individualized learning and literacy needs of bilingual and Spanish-speaking children. Specialized digital educational media can be used to teach language acquisition or to interpret a foreign language. Many digital apps provide opportunities for the user to change the language of both written and oral language in the software, accommodating the need for instruction or learning engagement in a home language. Other digital media provide self-paced learning experiences for children, offering individualized instruction. Using creative digital apps, children can design digital stories, songs, plays, and more that are both culturally relevant and in their language.

Digital picture books and digital storybook apps often have the functionality to change the printed language of the narrative, allowing the story to be read in different languages. Specific digital picture books and storybook apps can provide opportunities for children to hear a language read phonetically while words are highlighted, strengthening their literacy development. These types of digital media can be used by librarians to creatively extend their existing print collections and to acquire foreign-language materials to meet immediate needs of patrons. For instance, if a Spanish-speaking family moves to your community and you have few Spanish-language materials to offer, you could use the International Children's Digital Library (http://en.childrenslibrary.org/) or TumbleBooks (www.tumblebooklibrary.com/) to provide instant access to Spanish titles. If the family lacks connectivity at home and your library circulates digital tablets or computers with Internet access, family members could access these titles virtually. A more obvious use of digital picture books and storybook apps that we will discuss later is their incorporation into bilingual storytimes.

Context in which the librarian is using the digital media. The context in which a librarian uses a particular piece of digital media with a Latino or Spanish-speaking child is extremely important. Digital media should never be used as substitutes for bonding time between children and caregivers nor should media replace opportunities to interact with high-quality children's literature. Rather, digital apps, digital picture books, and other forms of digital media can be used to supplement or extend learning through interactive, hands-on creative exploration. Digital apps can be used to supplement whole-group learning in bilingual storytimes with modeling by the librarian using a digital tablet and projection system. Similarly, digital apps can serve as conduits for individual learning activities performed between caregivers and children after storytime.

Digital media interaction should not be a solo activity. Children need to be involved in joint media engagement with their peers, caregivers, family members, and librarians. Collaboratively, children should be exploring, learning, modeling, and creating. Studies show that when Latino and Spanish-speaking children are engaged in purposeful interaction with educational digital media, they are able to discuss and ask questions, participate in creative imaginative play and hands-on activities, or teach a caregiver something new related to the theme or content of the media. After enough purposeful exposure to relevant, meaningful digital media, Spanish-dominant children are often able to do all of the preceding in English while also reinforcing their home language through interactions with their caregivers.[8] Again, the key to digital media use is how the media are applied with these children in the bilingual storytime.

Child's developmental capabilities. Every child is unique in her language and literacy development. Although we can identify patterns of growth and development, the rate at which a child acquires a new language depends upon natural abilities and home environment. What may work for one child or one group of children may not be successful or relevant for other children. Children in supportive homes and those who have had previous shared learning experiences with a caregiver or older family member while reading a book or interacting with digital media will respond differently than children who have been left alone to use digital media. A child whose parent cuddles him while asking questions and prompting actions when using a digital app will be more likely to respond socially to digital media use in bilingual storytime than will a child who usually sits alone and struggles to use a digital app or digital storybook. Similarly, each child has unique interests that influence receptiveness to various forms of digital media. A creative app that involves making music might appeal more to a child who likes to physically create her own music by banging on pots than to a child who prefers to use toy trucks to build roads and bridges. A child who enjoys reading aloud with his grandmother might enjoy a storytelling app more so than a child who has limited or negative experiences with reading and storytelling.

It is important for librarians working with Latino and Spanish-speaking children to keep these differences in mind when planning bilingual storytimes and programs. If you incorporate digital media into your storytime and the effort is not successful, stop to consider why it did not work. The answer could lie in the way you used the digital media with the children, the individual and collective experiences and development of the children present at storytime, or the content of the digital media. Librarians would not think of abandoning books in bilingual storytime if one book was a flop with a group of children. The same holds true for digital media. Experiment with different types of digital media or different methods of sharing and find the ones that work for you. In figure 5.1 bilingual education scholar Karen Nemeth offers additional recommendations for librarians interested in using digital media with Latino and Spanish-speaking children. The free publication *Family Time with Apps: A Guide to Using Apps with Your Kids*, available in English and Spanish, is also a great resource for children's librarians to use with parents when explaining the educational uses of digital apps and assisting in the selection of quality digital apps to use at home.[9]

ROLE OF DIGITAL MEDIA IN BILINGUAL STORYTIMES

We have alluded to the use of digital media in bilingual storytimes, but exactly how can you purposefully supplement and complement your existing storytimes using digital media? You need not feel intimidated about the prospect. Digital apps and digital storybooks can be highlighted within a storytime much the same way as traditional print books and hands-on activities. A digital picture book or storybook app can be used in a digital storytime alongside other books on the same topic or theme. For instance, in a bilingual storytime about hair, you might use the Spanish/English bilingual digital storybook app *Curly Hair, Straight Hair* alongside culturally relevant picture books such as *Dalia's Wondrous Hair / El maravilloso cabello de Dalia* by Laura Lacámara or *Hairs / Pelitos* by Sandra Cisneros.[10] You can connect a digital tablet to the library's projection system, display the storybook app on the overhead screen, and then share the story with storytime attendees either by reading the story or by playing the Spanish narration of the story. Alternatively, you might load a bilingual storybook app on the library's digital tablets and encourage children and caregivers to read the story

FIGURE 5.1

KAREN NEMETH ON USING DIGITAL MEDIA WITH LATINO AND SPANISH-SPEAKING CHILDREN

KAREN NEMETH is a nationally recognized author, consultant, and scholar whose work focuses on first and second literacy and language acquisition of young children. She has written numerous articles, book chapters, and books related to using appropriate media with dual language learners. She firmly believes that when used appropriately, high-quality digital media and tablet technology can play an important role in the education of these children.

Karen's work focuses on using digital apps as well as digital media such as streaming YouTube videos along with digital tablets to explain a concept or communicate with children more effectively when there is a language barrier. She particularly advocates for using creative digital apps with Latino and Spanish-speaking children to allow them to record and use their own language. Karen notes, "It is not about finding a Spanish app to use with Spanish-speaking children. If I let children use an app where they can record their own voice, then they can use their own version of Spanish (dialect, regional, etc.) that is meaningful to them to facilitate their comprehension. It is important to focus on how digital media can be used to reach Latino families and how to get families and kids participating together in learning."

For librarians who are interested in using apps with Spanish-speaking families, Karen recommends starting with interactive, creative apps that offer compelling and unique technologies that will extend traditional storytime activities. For instance, she observes, "You can't have families record their voices over a paper book; but, if you have a storybook-making app, families can record their voices to hear the story in their own language. Technology in this instance is adding something that cannot be done any other way." Recommended apps that have this capability are Draw and Tell by Duck Duck Moose (www.duckduckmoose .com/educational-iphone-itouch-apps-for-kids/draw-and -tell/) and My Story (http://mystoryapp.org/).

"When a librarian intentionally uses a quality storybook app in bilingual storytime (which has recorded narration in correctly spoken English and Spanish)," Karen observes, "families are given the opportunity to hear and learn a new language." This allows librarians to create a program that is accessible to a multilingual group of children and caregivers. These apps can be used in both large and small groups depending on the goal of the storytime, the group in attendance, and the functionality of the app.

Karen emphasizes that apps do not replace traditional storytime activities. Rather, they add a language connection that can blend with other hands-on activities already used in bilingual storytimes. The Hispanic Information and Telecommunications Network's Early Learning Collaborative (ELC) program reinforces this idea through its Pocoyo apps meant to help young Spanish-speaking children with their English-language development, early literacy, and math skills. The ELC has developed a suite of transmedia learning resources that use digital media and hands-on games to extend learning. More information is available on the program's website (http://earlylearning collaborative.org/).

For the most part, Karen laments that apps with Latino content as well as apps with Spanish-language functionality are hard to find. "Story apps that make users go back to the home page and choose a language are problematic, particularly if instructions are in English." Many story apps that are bilingual use the same classic children's stories (such as The Three Bears) over and over, and very few focus on Latino culture. Also, with storybook apps, it is hard to find that one perfect app. "If you like the narration and don't like the pictures, you aren't going to use it. If you like the pictures but not the narration, you aren't going to use it either," Karen remarks.

App review websites can be overwhelming for educators, librarians, and caregivers. Karen does not have a recommended go-to resource for reviews of Spanish-language apps. She states, "I am very picky, and I never find anything that I really like. Children's Technology Review and Graphite are top review sources for apps, but both of them take time to read through and look for the rare find in Spanish. There is no way on a weekly basis to count on one resource to find something spectacular with Spanish-language capability. For the Spanish-speaking consumer there are language barriers. You have to get through the English reviews to find the Spanish stuff. If we could find more apps with user-friendly language access, rather than just e-books, that would be better."

Because of this dearth of truly exceptional Spanish-language apps, Karen advocates for the use of creative apps. She also encourages librarians and educators to push developers to give us what we need and, when possible, to create our own digital materials to use with Latino and Spanish-speaking children. "I have a file of great ideas for dual language apps," Karen relates, "but I need someone who can develop them. I can't do it!"

together at the end of storytime, either while waiting their turn for crafts or as a closing activity. The bilingual storybook app should have the functionality to sound out words for children and should include purposeful interactions such as singing that encourage playing with language. In addition to providing the preloaded digital tablets, you might want to circulate around the room to assist families in navigating the app. Other bilingual volunteers might also be useful to ensure all families receive help as needed.

Presenters can also use digital apps as learning tools during storytime. In a traditional storytime, you might use a feltboard to tell a story related to the program's theme. Anyone who has ever created feltboard pieces knows that it can take hours to create the various characters and props for a story. By using a digital app such as Felt Board, you can tell a story by dragging and dropping digital feltboard pieces on a digital feltboard much the same way as placing feltboard pieces on a real feltboard.[11] The visuals on the tablet look virtually the same as physical feltboard pieces. You can create your own backgrounds as well as characters with a variety of skin tones representing racial diversity. By connecting the digital tablet to the library projection system, you not only tell a feltboard story but also model how to use the digital app. After storytime, allow families to use tablets loaded with the Felt Board app to retell any of the stories shared during storytime or to create their own stories using their home language.

Songs are a staple of storytime and offer another opportunity for purposefully using digital media with bilingual children. The bilingual app Los Pollitos by Cantos teaches young children the popular Latin American song "Los Pollitos Dicen / Baby Chicks Sing."[12] The app offers several different choices for singers in both English and Spanish and includes hot spots (places for children to touch the screen) to make each chick sing "pío, pío, pío." Presenters can use the app to teach storytime attendees the song and to encourage young children to take turns making the chicks sing. The book Los Pollitos Dicen / The Baby Chicks Sing written by Nancy Abraham Hall and Jill Syverson-Stork could be included in a bilingual storytime with the app to introduce other Latin American nursery rhymes, or the bilingual e-book Los Pollitos by Andres Zapata could be shared to introduce the song in a story format.[13]

Another way to use digital apps in bilingual storytime is through a digital media extension activity that can be completed in the library or at home by the children and family members. This activity could include a bilingual, creative app where children can sing, tell a story, record their voice, or extend the program's theme in a creative capacity. The Sago Mini Doodlecast app, available in several different languages, is one example.[14] It supports literacy development through drawing and storytelling with the capability to record children's voices while they use story prompts to create a picture. Working alongside their caregivers or other family members, Latino and Spanish-speaking children can use the app to build upon the learning modeled in their bilingual storytime at the library.

Presenters might also include digital media in a bilingual storytime program through methods other than incorporating digital apps. For instance, Sparkup (http://sparkup.com/) is a digital tool that allows users to record and store audio versions of any children's book in any language. While an audio recording is being created, Sparkup's camera takes a photograph of the book's cover and of each page as it is being read. These images are archived along with the audio. Subsequently, when the Sparkup tool is connected to the book, it recognizes the front cover image and plays the audio recording stored for each page of the book. In a bilingual storytime, you might use a Sparkup device during an extension activity in which children and caregivers read (or retell the plot from) one of the stories you have shared. Recordings can also be stored in the library's Sparkup account and kept as part of a digital collection to be accessed at any time by library patrons. Recording alternative versions of a book in different languages and sharing them with children during storytime is another creative way to use Sparkup. If you want to share a specific title during storytime and that title is only available in English, then a trusted Spanish-speaking volunteer can create an audio translation of the text in Spanish using the Sparkup device. When you later share the book during storytime, connect the Sparkup tool to the physical book and, when the tool reads the book's cover image, Sparkup will play the Spanish version of the story. Children can listen to the story as a group or individually at a later time. Although this method should not be considered a substitute for using high-quality Spanish-language or bilingual titles, it does provide a creative solution for supplementing language acquisition.

Using these suggestions, you can easily incorporate digital media into any of the bilingual storytime models that we have shared in previous chapters. The following sample template is for a bilingual storytime incorporating digital media.

Sample Template: Bilingual Storytime with Digital Media

- Opening Song or Routine
- Bilingual or Spanish-Dominant Book
- Song or Movement Activity
- Bilingual or Spanish-Dominant Storybook App or Digital Picture Book
- Digital Learning Activity (use a thematic educational app with bilingual functionality to extend learning)
- Bilingual or Spanish-Dominant Book (optional)
- Closing Song or Routine
- Digital Media Extension Activity

For additional suggestions on integrating digital media into storytime, we recommend consulting *Young Children, New Media, and Libraries: A Guide for Incorporating New Media into Library Collections, Services, and Programs for Families and Children Ages 0–5* and *Diversity Programming for Digital Youth: Promoting Cultural Competence in the Children's Library.*[15] Librarians serving Latino and Spanish-speaking children can adapt most of the information from these books when planning bilingual digital storytimes.

SELECTING DIGITAL MEDIA

Choosing high-quality bilingual apps to use with children in bilingual storytimes is as important as selecting the right Spanish-language or bilingual book. The best digital apps are interactive, easy to navigate, purposeful, culturally affirming, free of grammatical and spelling errors, developmentally appropriate, and accessible. If an app has been developed to teach children a new language, the design should include the same or similar methodology and functionality used to teach and foster children's language and literacy in their primary language.

Unfortunately, there is little quality control in terms of the content and functionality of digital apps. It is more difficult for the average layperson to publish a bilingual children's book that might actually be widely available for use in a library. Unless they self-publish through platforms such as Amazon's CreateSpace, authors generally have to go through a rigorous process of working with an editor at a publishing house before their book is published and stocked in outlets where librarians purchase their collection materials. On the other hand, almost anyone with the right software can create a digital app for children and make it available for purchase through Google Play or Apple iTunes. No process exists to vet the quality of apps in terms of content, language use, functionality, design, developmental appropriateness, and cultural authenticity before the apps are available for librarians to purchase and use on digital tablets in storytimes. Therefore, it is imperative that librarians know how to evaluate bilingual apps for use in programming or know where to find reliable reviews. Figure 5.2 offers points to consider when choosing bilingual apps for use with children in storytimes, and figure 5.3 provides recommended review sources for digital apps and other digital media.

EXAMPLES OF BILINGUAL PROGRAMS USING DIGITAL MEDIA

To further assist librarians in the planning of bilingual storytimes using digital media, we provide examples of three bilingual literacy programs that either currently use digital media or have the potential for using digital media to reach out to Latino and Spanish-speaking children. We believe that each of these programs offers additional ideas that will spark creativity in your own digital bilingual storytimes. In figure 5.4, librarian Beatriz Guevara describes how the Charlotte Mecklenburg Library in Charlotte, North Carolina, uses digital media in storytimes and other programming with Spanish-speaking families.

FIGURE 5.2

CRITERIA FOR CHOOSING BILINGUAL APPS

Consider the languages available in the digital app.
- Are additional languages free?
- Are in-app purchases necessary to acquire an additional language for the app?
- Is it necessary to purchase a separate version of the app to acquire an additional language?

Examine the complexity and use of the language in the app.
- Are words presented one at a time, or are they used in age-appropriate sentences?
- Are isolated, low-value words used in the app with little meaning or purpose?
- Is language taught purposefully through stories and songs?
- Does the app include developmentally appropriate activities that require thought and response to introduce new vocabulary?

Scrutinize the accuracy of the app's language and cultural content.
- Was the app written in English and then translated? If so, are translations correct and culturally appropriate?
- Does the app developer provide documentation to support the accuracy of the translation?
- Is the entire app available in the two languages, or are specific portions such as instructions available in only one language?
- Are the images and activities culturally appropriate and free of stereotypes?

Determine the purpose of the app and assess whether it is developmentally appropriate.
- Does the app take a flash-card, rote memorization approach to teach a language?
- Does the app use engaging activities such as singing, creating, planning, or problem solving to teach a language?
- Is the purpose of the app to teach a new language, or is it simply a gaming, creative, or storybook app that is written in multiple languages?
- Does the app offer features to record users' language and to track progress of language development?
- How will the app supplement your bilingual storytime and engage children and their caregivers?

NOTE
We have adapted these criteria for librarians from Karen Nemeth, "Designing a Rubric for Preschool Bilingual Apps" (2012), www.ecetech.net/blog/dll/designing-a-rubric-for-preschool-bilingual-apps-by-karen-nemeth/.

FIGURE 5.3

REVIEW SOURCES FOR DIGITAL APPS AND OTHER DIGITAL MEDIA

- **Children's Technology Review:** http://childrenstech.com
- **Digital Storytime:** http://digital-storytime.com
- **Graphite:** www.graphite.org
- ***Horn Book* App Review of the Week:** www.hbook.com/category/choosing-books/app-review-of-the-week/
- ***Publishers Weekly* This Week in Children's Apps:** www.publishersweekly.com/pw/by-topic/digital/Apps/index.html
- ***School Library Journal* App Reviews:** www.slj.com/category/reviews/apps/
- **Teachers With Apps:** http://teacherswithapps.com

FIGURE 5.4

CASE STUDY | USING DIGITAL MEDIA IN PROGRAMMING WITH SPANISH-SPEAKING FAMILIES

BEATRIZ GUEVARA, the 2015–16 president of REFORMA (The National Association to Promote Library and Information Services to Latinos and the Spanish-Speaking), is the library manager at the Scaleybark Library, which is part of the Charlotte Mecklenburg Library system in Charlotte, North Carolina. She has also worked in another branch within the library system offering programs to the Spanish-speaking community. The branch provided computer classes, ESL (English as a second language) tutoring, and other programs for Spanish-speaking adults in addition to storytimes and Every Child Ready to Read workshops in Spanish for young children and their parents. The Spanish-speaking families that attended the weekly storytimes became a family of their own, referring to storytime as "la escuelita" (the little school) where both children and parents learned together. Beatriz planned as many learning opportunities and hands-on experiences as possible in the storytime. The children learned about U.S. and Latin American cultures, went on nature walks around the library, dressed up as their favorite book characters, and enjoyed musical and technology petting zoos.

Beatriz's branch had several iPads that she used in storytimes and early literacy workshops. Depending on the number of attendees during storytime, she would often introduce new words and concepts, such as colors, opposites, and letters, using the iPads. She would also use the digital tablet to play animal sounds as she mentioned them in her stories and to play music while storytelling to add suspense, romance, and playfulness. During the Every Child Ready to Read workshops, Beatriz created activities in which parents could develop the practices modeled in storytime with their children. As the families worked together, Beatriz would rotate iPads so that each family could use the device to practice writing, listen to animal sounds, engage in singing, or simply talk about a picture. Beatriz also downloaded multiple apps for children and parents to use together. These included creative apps featuring musical instruments that children could "play" and sing with their parents, painting apps in which children could use their fingers as a brush, and dress-up apps that allowed children to use their imagination as they created costumes.

Beatriz quickly noticed that many of the parents began to ask about using the iPads at the library with their older children. They often showed her letters from their children's teachers urging them to download apps and programs to help their school-age children with their math and reading. The volunteer tutors who helped children with their homework at the library were already using a laptop to conduct research for projects or to guide children in their writing. However, the children often did not interact with the device themselves. Beatriz instructed the tutors to begin working one-on-one with the children using the iPads at the end of each tutoring session. Tutors would load the apps or websites recommend by the child's teacher and let the child practice reading, spelling, or math skills through interactive games and stories. The children looked forward to each session because they saw the time with the iPad as a reward. The tutors were always there to provide support and assistance, but the time was a special new learning experience for the children.

Some of the families began to purchase iPads or other digital tablets to use at home and would come to the library for tutorials, tips, and app recommendations. However, most families could not afford to purchase the devices or the fee-based apps and preferred to continue using them at the library. "Unfortunately," Beatriz recalls, "most of the apps available were English only, which is often a challenge for Spanish-speaking parents who want to enjoy the game, story, [and the like] with their children. The children would get tired of interpreting for their parents and would tell them to 'just wait' until they were done. I definitely think that we need more bilingual apps in the market."

Beatriz also notes other uses of digital media within the library system. For instance, the Charlotte Mecklenburg Library has a website called StoryPlace: The Children's Digital Learning Library (storyplace.org), which features Spanish and English versions of stories and activities for young children. She suggests this site as one example of activities that could be used on digital tablets with Spanish-speaking children, particularly because the website is available in both languages. The ImaginOn branch in the library system has iPads with preloaded bilingual or Spanish-language apps available for parents to use. Beatriz further observes, "Throughout our system some of our bilingual storytellers are introducing these types of technologies to Spanish-speaking children, but there is still a lot of ground to cover for this population. It is our responsibility as librarians to provide these learning experiences for children that are willing to learn but may not have access to these devices at home. We must also advocate for more bilingual and Spanish print and digital materials to promote quality family time and cultural opportunities."

Día: El día de los niños / El día de los libros

Historically, many librarians conducting specialized bilingual storytimes[16] for Spanish-speaking and Latino families have used the celebration *El día de los niños / El día de los libros* or Children's Day / Book Day (Día for short) as a way to integrate Spanish-language materials and Latino cultural content into storytimes and other library programming. Although we advocate having regular, year-round bilingual storytimes, we acknowledge the opportunity for using Día as a springboard for general bilingual programming as well as storytimes using bilingual digital media.

Established twenty years ago by Latina children's author Pat Mora, Día combines elements of the international celebration Day of the Child with the celebration of reading enjoyment (Bookjoy) to promote bilingual literacy, highlight multicultural and global children's literature, and foster cultural understanding among all children and their families. Children's librarians across the nation have adopted the celebration, and each year REFORMA (The National Association to Promote Library and Information Services to Latinos and the Spanish-Speaking) bestows the Mora Award for exemplary Día programs. The Association for Library Service to Children (ALSC) provides an extensive website (http://dia.ala.org/) with recommendations of bilingual books, suggestions for Día programs and book clubs, and marketing materials in Spanish and English. Since its inception, Día (now also known as Diversity in Action) has expanded its focus to include a celebration of all languages and all cultures (not just Spanish-language and Latino culture), and we strongly support this concept to provide inclusive library programming that connects diverse cultures.

Librarians can go digital with Día to connect bilingual digital natives and their families with high-quality culturally and linguistically relevant digital media and children's books. In a Día program, a librarian could include both books and digital apps related to Latino and other cultures. A presenter might read the books *Mango, Abuela, and Me* (or the Spanish version, *Mango, Abuela y yo*) by Meg Medina and *Hot, Hot Roti for Dada-ji* by F. Zia and show the Tumble-Book digital picture book version of *I Love Saturdays y Domingos* by Alma Flor Ada using a digital tablet and the library's projection system.[17] All three books are about a child's relationship with his or her grandparents. A storytelling app, such as Bright Bot's My Story Book Creator or Enuma's Kid in Story Book Maker, could then be used to help children create their own stories about their grandparents.[18] These stories could be created after the Día program or as a digital media extension activity at home using circulated digital tablets. Stories could later be shared in the library during a subsequent bilingual storytime or library program. With its focus on intergenerational bonds and storytelling, this particular Día program holds cross-cultural appeal for numerous children and families and can be used to foster a sense of community within a library's service area. Additional ideas for using digital media in Día programs are available in the online archived presentation "Dynamic Digital Día: Promoting Cultural Competence in Digital Storytimes."[19]

Comienza en Casa / It Starts at Home

Launched in 2012 and developed by the Maine Migrant Education Program and the nonprofit organization Mano en Mano / Hand in Hand, Comienza en Casa / It Starts at Home is a digital literacy program for migrant Latino families in rural Maine. Incorporating hands-on activities, children's literature, digital books, educational and creative digital apps, and structured family conversations, the program facilitates school readiness and literacy skills for young Spanish-speaking children with limited English proficiency. Designed by mother-daughter team Bonnie and Ana Blagojevic, the curriculum includes the following components: read, structured play, create, offscreen activity, family focus, and free play. Each component is described in the following paragraphs.

The first component of the Comienza en Casa curriculum is *read*. Children and caregivers read a Spanish translation of an English book from the curriculum focusing on topics such as concepts, the environment, and relationships. Depending on the age and language proficiency of the child, either the caregiver reads the book to the child or the child reads the book to a family member. Occasionally a digital picture book or storybook app is used along with a print book. A portion of the training for the program includes online instructional video clips in Spanish and English for caregivers related to shared reading and family literacy. These videos are part of the Family Reading Time program (www1.easternct.edu/cece/family-reading-time/) developed by the Dialogic Reading for Multilingual Families project at Eastern Connecticut State University. This project offers training to multilingual families on the importance of shared reading in the first language of the child.

Structured play is the next component of the curriculum. In this step, the caregiver and child explore an educational app together, with the child leading and caregiver assisting. These basic, concept-based apps are available in English or Spanish and expand on the theme or concept introduced in the children's book. Suggested topics and scaffolding questions are supplied to encourage interaction between the child and caregiver.

The third component of the Comienza en Casa curriculum is *create*. Families explore an interactive, creative app with the child leading and caregiver assisting. Question prompts provide scaffolding of previously introduced concepts, and in-app activities are also suggested. Creative apps can include drawing, storytelling, music, voiceover, and the like.

The fourth area of the curriculum is *offscreen activity*. With the assistance of caregivers, children actively participate in several hands-on activities that involve movement, crafts, science experiments, and so on. The purpose of this program element is to have children engage in activities that build upon previous learning but are not tied to a digital device. As the program has progressed, many of these activities have included STEM (science, technology, engineering, and math) components.

An integral component for the program's success is *family focus*, which encompasses training caregivers on how to model early literacy activities and foster second-language development. Online early literacy resources in English with Spanish translations are provided and include materials from Reading Is Fundamental, ¡Colorín Colorado!, and the National Association for the Education of Young Children (NAEYC). Caregivers are also provided with digital tablets preloaded with video clips in Spanish and English from ReadyRosie (http://readyrosie.com/) that model early literacy interactions between caregivers and children. The intent is for caregivers to watch the video clips and then repeat the actions with their children.

The final area of the curriculum is *free play*, in which children are encouraged to engage in unstructured free play with interactive gaming and creative apps. A list of interactive apps is provided for children to explore either independently or with their family. Uninhibited play allows them to further explore concepts or themes in the curriculum through a lens that meets their individual interests and developmental needs.

Librarians can find information about Comienza en Casa, including recommended digital apps, videos, samples of children's work, and archives of the curriculum, on the program's website (www.manomaine.org/programs/mep/comienzaencasa). A vignette that successfully demonstrates the effectiveness of the program in helping Spanish-speaking children with English-language fluency is available in *Tap, Click, Read: Growing Readers in a World of Screens*.[20] The Comienza en Casa program holds significant potential as a model for children's librarians if it is modified to include bilingual children's books and apps with relevant Latino cultural content. As with a traditional bilingual storytime, it is imperative to include activities that allow children and their parents to play with language and explore their own cultures and cultures different from their own.

Mother Goose on the Loose en Español

Beginning as Buena Casa, Buena Brasa (A Warm Home, A Warm Hearth), Mother Goose on the Loose (MGOL) en Español was created by Betsy Diamant-Cohen with the help of Anne Calderón as a Spanish-language version of the Mother Goose on the Loose early literacy program. MGOL en Español is a dynamic, research-based library program for young bilingual and Spanish-speaking children and their caregivers that uses culturally relevant rhymes, literature, and repetition to reinforce early literacy skills. Numerous libraries serving Latino and Spanish-speaking children and families use the MGOL en Español curriculum by either presenting it in separate programs or incorporating elements into bilingual storytimes. In 2013, Diamant-Cohen made elements of the program digital with the creation of the digital app Felt Board Mother Goose on the Loose.[21] Designed by the same software company that created the Felt Board app, this app resembles an actual feltboard with manipulative pieces and can be used for storytelling and interactive play. The app also includes a section for parents on how to extend early literacy learning beyond the app through rhymes, reading, and creative play.

Librarians can easily use the digital app to supplement the regular program plans and suggested activities of the MGOL en Español curriculum mentioned in the book *Early Literacy Programming en Español: Mother Goose on the Loose Programs for Bilingual Learners.*[22] By using this predesigned curriculum for bilingual children, librarians initially testing the waters with digital apps in storytimes may find the task less daunting. In addition, because Diamant-Cohen is a well-respected advocate for early childhood literacy, her endorsement of an app in bilingual storytime to facilitate child and parent bonding can help sway more reluctant librarians. Additional information about using the digital app within the existing MGOL program is available in the "MGOL and New Media" section of the MGOL website (www.mgol.net/about/mgol-and-technology/mgol-and-new-media/).

CONCLUDING THOUGHTS

The inclusion of digital media in bilingual storytimes can be a wonderful way to reach out to Latino and Spanish-speaking families who might not otherwise attend a library program or who have limited access to digital technologies. Librarians who purposefully choose high-quality digital apps or digital picture books to accompany dynamic read-aloud books in a storytime have the power to create dynamic literacy experiences that not only foster language development but also promote lifelong learning in new and exciting ways. Bilingual digital storytimes provide unique opportunities for children's librarians to serve as media mentors, helping Latino and Spanish-speaking parents learn how to select and use the best digital media in meaningful ways with their children.

Although many librarians may be hesitant to include digital media in bilingual storytimes or endorse digital apps for fear of betraying the printed word, we hope that you will stop and consider the important role that you can play in the lives of Latino and Spanish-speaking families. Keep an open mind, and dream of the possibilities. We love books, but we also appreciate the potential of purposeful and quality digital media in bilingual storytime. We hope you will too!

NOTES

1. June Lee and Brigid Barron, "Aprendiendo en Casa: Media as a Learning Tool among Hispanic-Latino Families," The Joan Ganz Cooney Center at Sesame Workshop (February 2015), www.joanganzcooneycenter.org/publication/aprendiendo-en-casa-media-as-a-learning-tool-among-hispanic-latino-families; Bruce Fuller, José Ramón Lizárraga, and James Gray, "Digital Media and Latino Families: New Channels for Learning, Parenting, and Organizing," The Joan Ganz Cooney Center at Sesame Workshop (February 2015), www.joanganzcooneycenter.org/publication/digital-media-and-latino-families-new-channels-for-learning-parenting-and-organizing/.

2. Lee and Barron, "Aprendiendo en Casa"; Fuller, Lizárraga, and Gray, "Digital Media and Latino Families"; Mark Hugo Lopez, Ana Gonzalez-Barrera, and Eileen Patten, "Closing the Digital Divide: Latinos and Technology Adoption," Pew Research Center, Hispanic Trends Project (March 2013), www.pewhispanic.org/2013/03/07/closing-the-digital-divide-latinos-and-technology-adoption/.

3. Lee and Barron, "Aprendiendo en Casa."

4. Fuller, Lizárraga, and Gray, "Digital Media and Latino Families."

5. Vikki Katz and Michael Levine, "Connecting to Learn: Promoting Digital Equity for America's Hispanic Families," The Joan Ganz Cooney Center at Sesame Workshop (February 2015), www.joanganzcooneycenter.org/publication/connecting-to-learn-promoting-digital-equity-for-americas-hispanic-families/.

6. Cen Campbell, Claudia Haines, Amy Koester, and Dorothy Stoltz, "Media Mentorship in Libraries Serving Youth" [White Paper], Association for Library Service to Children (adopted March 2015), www.ala.org/alsc/mediamentorship.

7. Lisa Guernsey, *Screen Time: How Electronic Media—From Baby Videos to Educational Software—Affects Your Young Child* (New York: Basic Books, 2012).

8. Lee and Barron, "Aprendiendo en Casa"; Katz and Levine, "Connecting to Learn."

9. The Joan Ganz Cooney Center at Sesame Workshop, "Family Time with Apps: A Guide to Using Apps with Your Kids" (December 2014), www.joanganzcooneycenter.org/publication/family-time-with-apps/; Spanish version: "Apps en familia: Guía para usar apps con tus hijos" (August 2015), www.joanganzcooneycenter.org/publication/apps-en-familia-guia-para-usar-apps-con-tus-hijos/.

10. 33 Loretta Kids' Books LLC, *Curly Hair, Straight Hair* (2011), https://itunes.apple.com/us/app/curly-hair-straight-hair/id469512365?mt=8; Laura Lacámara, *Dalia's Wondrous Hair / El maravilloso cabello de Dalia* (Houston, TX: Piñata Books, 2014); Sandra Cisneros, *Hairs / Pelitos* (New York: Dragonfly Books, 1997).

11. Software Smoothie, Felt Board (2014), https://itunes.apple.com/us/app/felt-board/id492342753?mt=8.

12. Cantos, Los Pollitos (2012), https://itunes.apple.com/us/app/los-pollitos/id527097576?mt=8.

13. Nancy Abraham Hall, Jill Syverson-Stork, and Kay Chorao, *Los Pollitos Dicen / The Baby Chicks Sing* (New York: Little, Brown, 1994); Andres Zapata, *Los Pollitos* (Broomall, PA: Mason Reads, 2012).

14. Sago, Sago Mini Doodlecast (2013), https://itunes.apple.com/app/sago-mini-doodlecast/id469487373?mt=8.

15. Amy Koester, ed., *Young Children, New Media, and Libraries: A Guide for Incorporating New Media into Library Collections, Services, and Programs for Families and Children Ages 0–5* (San Francisco: Little eLit 2015), http://littleelit.com/book/; Jamie Campbell Naidoo, *Diversity Programming for Digital Youth: Promoting Cultural Competence in the Children's Library* (Santa Barbara, CA: Libraries Unlimited, 2014).

16. The term *specialized bilingual storytimes* indicates those bilingual storytime programs that are offered sporadically or once a year rather than regularly.

17. Meg Medina and Angela Dominguez, *Mango, Abuela, and Me* (Boston: Candlewick, 2015); F. Zia and Ken Min, *Hot, Hot Roti for Dada-ji* (New York: Lee and Low Books, 2011); Alma Flor Ada and Elivia Savadier, *I Love Saturdays y Domingos* (TumbleBook version: http://preview.tumblebooks.com/book.aspx?id=3117).

18. Bright Bot, My Story Book Creator (2015), https://itunes.apple.com/us/app/my-story
-book-creator-school/id449232368?mt=8; Enuma, Kid in Story Book Maker (2014),
https://itunes.apple.com/us/app/kid-in-story-book-maker-create/id594403164?mt=8.
Another recommended resource for storytelling digital apps for bilingual children or
English language learners is Erin Wilkey Oh's "6 Storytelling Apps That Get English
Language Learners Talking," KQED News (August 31, 2015), http://ww2.kqed.org/
mindshift/2015/08/31/6-storytelling-apps-that-get-english-language-learners
-talking/.

19. Jamie Campbell Naidoo, Cen Campbell, and Karen Nemeth, "Dynamic Digital Día:
Promoting Cultural Competence in Digital Storytimes" (July 2014), www.slideshare
.net/CenCampbell/dynamic-digital-dia-promoting-cultural-competence-in
-digital-storytimes.

20. Lisa Guernsey and Michael Levine, *Tap, Click, Read: Growing Readers in a World of
Screens* (San Francisco: Jossey-Bass, 2015). Additional profiles of Comienza en Casa
are available on the program's website, www.manomaine.org/programs/mep/
comienzaencasa/resources.

21. Software Smoothie, Felt Board—Mother Goose on the Loose (2013), https://itunes
.apple.com/us/app/felt-board-mother-goose-on/id734913054?mt=8.

22. Betsy Diamant-Cohen, *Early Literacy Programming en Español: Mother Goose on the
Loose Programs for Bilingual Learners* (New York: Neal-Schuman, 2010).

Part Two
RESOURCE MATERIALS

Chapter Six

Ready-to-Use Bilingual Program Plans

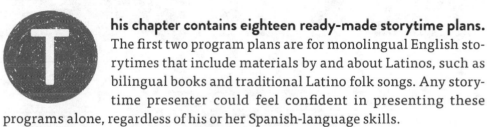

This chapter contains eighteen ready-made storytime plans. The first two program plans are for monolingual English storytimes that include materials by and about Latinos, such as bilingual books and traditional Latino folk songs. Any storytime presenter could feel confident in presenting these programs alone, regardless of his or her Spanish-language skills.

The remaining sixteen program plans offer bilingual storytimes for various ages, organized by theme. These programs are designed for presenters who are bilingual or who are working in tandem with a bilingual partner. The two programs for babies focus on providing lots of opportunities for adult–child interaction and incorporate many traditional and translated songs and rhymes. The three programs for toddlers and the six programs for preschool-age children include more books and storytelling as well as suggested extension activities. Five highly interactive mixed-age programs are also included for families who are bringing children of multiple ages to the library to enjoy storytime together. Programs are designed so that presenters can allow their own storytime style to influence the various elements of presentation, such as whether English and Spanish are used simultaneously or separately. It is our hope that these program plans, rather than being rigid guides, will inspire presenters to experiment and to incorporate their own creative ideas. Strong emphasis is placed on using bilingual books and books by Latino authors and illustrators, though some translated versions of English-language titles are also used. Each program plan ends with several additional recommended materials that correspond with the program theme and relevant online resources that librarians may want to explore themselves or share with parents. In some instances, we have also recommended digital apps that can be either incorporated into the program or used as a supplementary learning activity.

AGE
RANGE
Mixed Age /
Family

PROGRAM TITLE	DEVELOPED BY	THEME
Familia Fun	Katie Scherrer	Family / La familia

Note: This is an example of an English-language program that celebrates Latino culture and the Spanish language. With modifications, bilingual presenters or partners could present this program as a truly bilingual storytime as well.

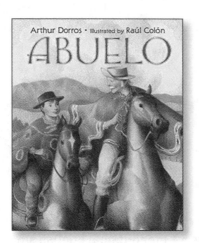

Opening Routine

Sing to the tune of "She'll Be Coming 'Round the Mountain."

Hello Friends, Hola Amigos

Hello friends, hello friends, how are you?
Hola amigos, hola amigos, ¿cómo están?
Hello friends, how are you?
Hola amigos, ¿cómo están?
Hello friends, hola amigos, how are you?

Hola amigos, we are here for storytime.
Hola amigos, we are here for storytime.
Hello friends, hola amigos.
We'll share stories, we'll share cuentos.
Hola amigos, we are here for storytime.

Book

Abuelo by Arthur Dorros, illustrated by Raúl Colón
> ❯ A boy learns important life lessons while riding horses with his grandfather on the South American plains.

Movement Song

"Muévete" from *From Here to There* by Nathalia Palis (CD)
> ❯ This energetic, bilingual song will get the whole family moving!

Book

Somos primos / We Are Cousins by Diane Gonzales Bertrand, illustrated by Christina E. Rodriguez
> ❯ This bilingual book introduces the extended family members who are often best friends growing up—cousins!

Movement Song

This is a bilingual adaptation of a traditional Spanish-language children's song. Move the various body parts as you sing along.

La tía Monica

Refrain
I have a sweet old tía
Her name is Monica
And when she goes out dancing
They all say, "Ooh la la!"
"Ooh la la!" "Ooh la la!"
They all say, "Ooh la la!"

She moves her feet like this,
like this, like this, like this.
Así se mueve los pies,
así, así, así.

Repeat refrain.

She moves her knees like this,
like this, like this, like this.
Así se mueve las rodillas,
así, así, así.

Repeat refrain.

She moves her hips like this,
like this, like this, like this.
Así se mueve las caderas,
así, así, así.

Repeat refrain.

She moves her shoulders like this,
like this, like this, like this.
Así se mueve los hombros,
así, así, así.

Repeat refrain.

She moves her head like this,
like this, like this, like this.
Así se mueve la cabeza,
así, así, así.

Repeat refrain.

Book

Sweet Dreams / Dulces sueños by Pat Mora, illustrated by Maribel Suárez
  ● Abuela tucks in each child in the family at the end of the day and wishes each one goodnight in this tender story.

Closing Routine

"Adiós" from *Playtime Spanish for Kids* by Beth Manners (CD)

Extension Activity

Family Footprints

Have children and caregivers trace their feet on pieces of butcher paper or large sheets of construction paper. Caregivers and children can cut out the paper feet together and then write their names on the feet. Each family can put their feet in order from smallest to largest. Depending on group size, you may try putting everyone's feet in order from smallest to largest! This is a modified version of a family activity from PBS Kids Lab (http://pbskids.org/lab/activity/familyfeet/).

- Butcher paper or large sheets of construction paper
- Markers or crayons
- Scissors

Bonus Storytime Resources

Dear Primo: A Letter to My Cousin by Duncan Tonatiuh
> ❯ Cousins from Mexico and the United States share letters and learn how their lives are similar and different.

Hairs / Pelitos by Sandra Cisneros, illustrated by Terry Ybáñez, translated by Liliana Valenzuela
> ❯ This is a beautiful comparison of the different types of hair in one girl's family.

Papá and Me by Arthur Dorros, illustrated by Rudy Gutierrez
> ❯ A little boy enjoys a special day in the city with his papá.

Relevant Websites

King County Library System: Tell Me a Story—Tía Monica
http://tmas.kcls.org/tia-monica-the-ooo-la-la-dancing-song/
> ❯ An English-language video demonstration of this traditional song.

PBS Kids Lab: Los pies de la familia
http://pbskids.org/lab/es/activity/familyfeet/
> ❯ Spanish instructions for an extended version of the "Family Footprints" activity.

AGE
RANGE
Mixed Age /
Family

PROGRAM TITLE	DEVELOPED BY	THEME
¡Arroz con leche! Rice Pudding!	Katie Scherrer	Dessert / El postre

Note: This is an example of an English-language program that celebrates Latino culture and the Spanish language. With modifications, bilingual presenters or partners could present this program as a truly bilingual storytime as well.

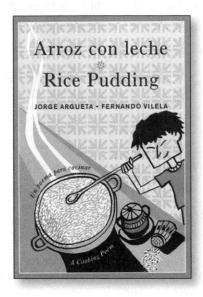

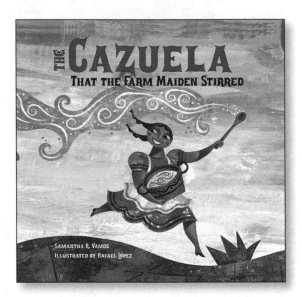

Opening Routine

Sing to the tune of "She'll Be Coming 'Round the Mountain."

Hello Friends, Hola Amigos

Hello friends, hello friends, how are you?
Hola amigos, hola amigos, ¿cómo están?
Hello friends, how are you?
Hola amigos, ¿cómo están?
Hello friends, hola amigos, how are you?

Hola amigos, we are here for storytime.
Hola amigos, we are here for storytime.
Hello friends, hola amigos.
We'll share stories, we'll share cuentos.
Hola amigos, we are here for storytime.

Movement Song

"Frota tu Panza" from *ABC Fiesta* by Mister G (CD)
> ● Move along to the motions in this bilingual song! Talk about the vocabulary for the various parts of the body before playing the song. If you feel comfortable, introduce the same body vocabulary in Spanish. Note that the movements in the Spanish parts of the song are different from those in the English parts of the song. The accompanying chart has a quick guide:

Spanish Phrases in "Frota tu Panza"	English Meanings
Frota tu panza	Rub your tummy
Toca tu nariz	Touch your nose
Toca tus pies	Touch your toes
Toca tus orejas	Touch your ears
Toca tus rodillas	Touch your knees

Book

The Cazuela That the Farm Maiden Stirred by Samantha Vamos, illustrated by Rafael López
> ● In this cumulative tale, all the animals on the farm pitch in to help the maiden make arroz con leche for a fiesta. Spanish words are incorporated and repeated throughout the text.

Traditional Song

"Arroz con leche" from *Juguemos a Cantar: Baby's First Songs in Spanish* (CD)
> ● Many versions of this traditional song are available. This version is particularly upbeat and fun to use with egg shakers or other musical instruments or for parachute play.

Book

Arroz con leche: Un poema para cocinar / Rice Pudding: A Cooking Poem by Jorge Argueta, illustrated by Fernando Vilela
> ● A whimsical bilingual poem that walks readers through the process of making arroz con leche. Read the English version of the poem, incorporating the names of the various ingredients in Spanish as you go along.

Closing Routine

"Adiós" from *Playtime Spanish for Kids* by Beth Manners (CD)

Extension Activity

Making Arroz con Leche!

INSTRUCTIONS

Following the recipe in *Arroz con leche: Un poema para cocinar / Rice Pudding: A Cooking Poem* by Jorge Argueta, bring examples of the ingredients used to make rice pudding. Have children and families help measure the various ingredients to practice math skills such as measuring and comparing. If possible, provide a premade sample of arroz con leche for families to try following this activity. Encourage adults to use lots of words as they interact with their child(ren) to describe the rice pudding.

MATERIALS NEEDED

- Measuring cups and spoons
- A large pot
- Play stove (if available)
- Various ingredients used to make rice pudding (such as rice, milk, sugar, and cinnamon)

Bonus Storytime Resources

Arroz con leche: Popular Songs and Rhymes from Latin America by Lulu Delacre
   ❷ Select and share a few rhymes from this wonderful bilingual collection. Two suggested rhymes that are widely known and easy to sing even with limited Spanish skills are "¡Qué llueva!" and "Un elefante se balanceaba." Demonstrations of both are available from StoryBlocks at www.storyblocks.org/videos/language/espanol/ (search for "¡Qué llueva!" and "Los elefantes").

¿Qué puedes hacer con una paleta? / What Can You Do with a Paleta? by Carmen Tafolla, illustrated by Magaly Morales
   ❷ This vibrant bilingual book celebrates another dessert, the fruity popsicle known in Spanish as a paleta.

Relevant Websites

Mister G: ABC Fiesta Songbook
www.mistergsongs.com/wp-content/uploads/2015/02/ABC-FIESTA
   -Songbook-.pdf
   ❯ Find song lyrics and tips for how to use the songs from this CD.

Children's Museum of Houston: Para los Niños—Healthy Minds, Healthy Bodies
www.cmhouston.org/healthy-minds-healthy-bodies
   ❯ A collection of family literacy activities on the theme of healthy eating, available in English and Spanish.

PROGRAM TITLE	DEVELOPED BY	THEME
¡Bebés juguetones! / Bouncing Babies!	Katie Scherrer	Let's Play! / ¡A jugar!

AGE RANGE
Babies

Opening Routine

Sitting together in a circle, go around the group asking "What's your name? ¿Cómo te llamas?" Chant or sing (to your own tune) this rhyme in English and Spanish to each child to welcome everyone to storytime. Have caregivers help children clap the syllables in each child's name.

What's Your Name?	¿Cómo te llamas?
Her (His) name is (name), (name), (name).	Se llama (nombre), (nombre), (nombre).
Her (His) name is (name).	Se llama (nombre).
What's your name?	¿Cómo te llamas?

Traditional Rhyme

Repeat this rhyme twice in both Spanish and English, tapping your legs as you go along. Rather than being a literal translation, the English version has a rhythm and rhyme pattern similar to the original Spanish rhyme.

Tortillitas	Little Tortillas
Tortillitas de manteca	Little tortillas made of wheat
para mamá que está contenta.	For my mom who is so sweet.
Tortillitas de salvado	Little tortillas made of corn
para papá que está enojado.	For my dad who I adore!

Counting Rhyme

Adults can help babies count along on their fingers in Spanish and English as you share this rhyme.

Diez deditos	Ten Little Fingers
Dos manitas, diez deditos.	Two little hands and ten little fingers.
Dos manitas, diez deditos.	Two little hands and ten little fingers.
Dos manitas, diez deditos.	Two little hands and ten little fingers.
Cuéntenlos conmigo.	Count them with me now.
Uno, dos, tres deditos,	One little, two little, three little fingers,
cuatro, cinco, seis deditos,	Four little, five little, six little fingers,
siete, ocho, nueve deditos,	Seven little, eight little, nine little fingers,
¡diez deditos son!	Ten little fingers all!

Book

Fiesta Babies by Carmen Tafolla, illustrated by Amy Córdova
  ◉ A sweet, rhyming story in which fiesta babies enjoy a celebration.

One-on-One Reading Time

Provide board books so adult caregivers and children can spend a few minutes reading together. A recommended bilingual board book series is the ArteKids! series created by the San Antonio Museum of Art. Colorful, bilingual board books explore first concepts such as shapes, colors, and numbers.

Free Play

Provide age-appropriate props that babies can play with freely while listening to music. Balls, soft toys, or puppets will work well for this activity. Walkers can move about the room and play, while adults can interact with children who aren't yet walking. A recommended bilingual song for this type of free play is "Animal Bop" from *From Here to There* by Nathalia Palis (CD).

Cleanup Song

Sing this simple song as you encourage the children to help you put away any toys or manipulatives used during free play.

Limpia	Clean Up
Limpia, limpia.	Clean up, clean up.
Guarda todo en su lugar.	It's time to put our things away.
Limpia, limpia.	Clean up, clean up.
Guarda todo en su lugar.	It's time to put our things away.

Traditional Rhyme

Adults can help babies make the motions of this rhyme with their hands.

Open, Shut Them	Ábranlas, ciérrenlas
Open, shut them. Open, shut them.	Ábranlas, ciérrenlas. Ábranlas, ciérrenlas.
Give a little clap, clap, clap.	Pla, pla, pla, pla, pla.
Open, shut them. Open, shut them.	Ábranlas, ciérrenlas. Ábranlas, ciérrenlas.
Lay them in your lap, lap, lap.	Pónganlas acá.
Walk them, walk them. Walk them, walk them.	Camínenlas, camínenlas, camínenlas, camínenlas,
Right up to your chin, chin, chin.	hasta la carita.
Walk them, walk them. Walk them, walk them.	Camínenlas, camínenlas, camínenlas, camínenlas,
Do not let them in, in, in.	¡cuidado! ¡No entren en la boquita!
Open, shut them. Open, shut them.	Ábranlas, ciérrenlas. Ábranlas, ciérrenlas.
Give a little clap, clap, clap.	Pla, pla, pla, pla, pla.
Open, shut them. Open, shut them.	Ábranlas, ciérrenlas. Ábranlas, ciérrenlas.
Lay them in your lap, lap, lap.	Pónganlas acá.

Traditional Rhyme

Have adults walk their fingers along their baby's arms and legs while sharing this rhyme. Adults can give a tickle each time the little mouse runs around the house! Repeat twice in each language.

The Snail and the Mouse	El caracol y la ratoncita
Slowly, slowly, slowly	Despacito, despacito
Creeps the garden snail.	se mueve el caracol.
Slowly, slowly, slowly	Despacito, muy despacito
Up the wooden rail.	a saludar al sol.
Quickly, quickly, quickly	Rápidamente, rápidamente
Runs the little mouse.	corre la ratoncita.
Quickly, quickly, quickly	Rápidamente, muy rápidamente
All around the house.	por toda la casita.

Closing Routine

Sing in English and Spanish to the tune of "She'll Be Coming 'Round the Mountain."

It's Time to Say Goodbye	Es tiempo a decir adiós
It's time to say goodbye to all our friends.	Es tiempo a decir adiós a los amigos.
It's time to say goodbye to all our friends.	Es tiempo a decir adiós a los amigos.
It's time to say goodbye, it's time to say goodbye.	Es tiempo a decir adiós, es tiempo a decir adiós.
It's time to say goodbye to all our friends.	Es tiempo a decir adiós a los amigos.

Bonus Storytime Resources

¡Pío Peep! Rimas tradicionales en español / Traditional Spanish Nursery Rhymes selected by Alma Flor Ada and F. Isabel Campoy, illustrated by Viví Escrivá, English translations by Alice Schertle
- ❯ A wonderful bilingual collection of children's rhymes.

Cantaba la rana / The Frog Was Singing by Rita Rosa Ruesga, illustrated by
Soledad Sebastián
> A bilingual collection of children's songs, which includes musical nota-
tions. All of the songs in the book can be listened to or downloaded at www
.scholastic.com/browse/book.jsp?id=1313837.

Relevant Websites

Association for Library Service to Children: Babies Need Words Every Day
www.ala.org/alsc/babiesneedwords
> Multiple downloadable posters in English and Spanish about the
importance of talking, singing, reading, and playing with babies daily.

Reading Is Fundamental: Juegos digitales
www.rif.org/books-activities/juegos-digitales/
> Videos of several Spanish fingerplays for babies.

YouTube: Library of Virginia—El caracol y la ratoncita / The Snail and
the Mouse
www.youtube.com/watch?v=f8iJVD_2q_E
> A video demonstration of this children's rhyme.

PROGRAM TITLE	DEVELOPED BY	THEME	
¡Bebés juguetones! / Bouncing Babies!	Katie Scherrer	Body / El cuerpo	AGE RANGE Babies

Opening Routine

Sitting together in a circle, go around the group asking, "What's Your Name? ¿Cómo te llamas?" Chant or sing (to your own tune) this rhyme in English and Spanish to each child to welcome everyone to storytime. Have caregivers help children clap the syllables in each child's name.

What's Your Name?	¿Cómo te llamas?
Her (His) name is (name), (name), (name).	Se llama (nombre), (nombre), (nombre).
Her (His) name is (name).	Se llama (nombre).
What's your name?	¿Cómo te llamas?

Traditional Rhyme

Adults can help baby find each hand as you share this rhyme. Repeat twice in each language.

Saco una manita	I Take Out My Little Hand
Saco una manita, la hago bailar,	I take out my little hand, I make it dance and play,
la abro, la cierro y la vuelvo a guardar.	I open it, I close it, I put it back away.
Saco la otra manita, la hago bailar,	I take out my other hand, I make it dance and play,
la abro, la cierro y la vuelvo a guardar.	I open it, I close it, I put it back away.
Saco las dos manitas, las hago bailar,	I take out both little hands, I make them dance and play,
las abro, las cierro y las vuelvo a guardar.	I open them, I close them, I put them back away.

Piggyback Song

Sing to the tune of "Twinkle, Twinkle, Little Star." Spanish lyrics from ¡A Bailar! Let's Dance! Spanish Learning Songs by Jorge Anaya (CD), available at www.whistle fritz.com/wp-content/uploads/2015/02/bailar-booklet-download.pdf. Note that the English version has been modified to maintain rhythm and rhyme and is not an exact translation.

Ojos, orejas	Eyes and Ears
Ojos, orejas,	Eyes and ears,
boca y nariz.	Mouth and nose.
Cara y dientes,	When I am happy,
una sonrisa.	My smile grows.

Book

Where Is Baby's Belly Button? by Karen Katz; translated by Argentina Palacios
 Ziegler as *¿Dónde está el ombliguito?*
   ❯ Lift the flaps to find various parts of Baby's body.

One-on-One Reading Time

Provide board books so adult caregivers and children can spend a few minutes reading together. A recommended bilingual board book series is Lil' Libros by Patty Rodriguez and illustrated by Ariana Stein. These bilingual first concept books playfully incorporate figures and traditions from Mexican culture.

Free Play

Provide age-appropriate props that babies can play with freely while listening to music. Balls, soft toys, or puppets will work well for this activity. Walkers can move about the room and play, while adults can interact with children who aren't yet walking. A recommended bilingual song for this type of free play is "Animal Bop" from *From Here to There* by Nathalia Palis (CD).

Cleanup Song

Sing this simple song as you encourage the children to help you put away any toys or manipulatives used during free play.

Limpia	Clean Up
Limpia, limpia.	Clean up, clean up.
Guarda todo en su lugar.	It's time to put our things away.
Limpia, limpia.	Clean up, clean up.
Guarda todo en su lugar.	It's time to put our things away.

Tickle Rhyme

With kisses and tickles, adult caregivers can help babies find the various parts of the body. Note that the Spanish version has been modified to maintain rhythm and rhyme and is not an exact translation.

One to Five[1]	Uno a cinco
One little nose,	Una nariz,
Two little feet,	dos manitas,
Three little tickles on your tummy so sweet!	¡tres cosquillas en la barriguita!
Four little kisses on five little toes,	Cuatro besitos en cinco deditos,
Then one more kiss for your sweet little nose!	para bebé, ¡un abracito!

Traditional Rhyme

This traditional rhyme has been modified to create a version that works in both English and Spanish. Adults help babies do the motions as you clap along.

Teddy Bear, Teddy Bear	Osito, Osito
Teddy Bear, Teddy Bear, turn around.	Osito, Osito, da la vuelta.
Teddy Bear, Teddy Bear, touch the ground.	Osito, Osito, toca la tierra.
Teddy Bear, Teddy Bear, clap your hands, please.	Osito, Osito, aplaude las manitas.
Teddy Bear, Teddy Bear, touch your knees.	Osito, Osito, toca las rodillas.
Teddy Bear, Teddy Bear, arms out wide.	Osito, Osito, los brazos abiertos.
Teddy Bear, Teddy Bear, jump up high.	Osito, Osito, saltos y saltos.
Teddy Bear, Teddy Bear, sit back down.	Osito, Osito, siéntate en el suelo.
Teddy Bear, Teddy Bear, it's time to rest now.	Osito, Osito, es hora de descansar.

Closing Routine

Sing in English and Spanish to the tune of "She'll Be Coming 'Round the Mountain."

It's Time to Say Goodbye	Es tiempo a decir adiós
It's time to say goodbye to all our friends.	Es tiempo a decir adiós a los amigos.
It's time to say goodbye to all our friends.	Es tiempo a decir adiós a los amigos.
It's time to say goodbye, it's time to say goodbye.	Es tiempo a decir adiós, es tiempo a decir adiós.
It's time to say goodbye to all our friends.	Es tiempo a decir adiós a los amigos.

Bonus Storytime Resources

Diez deditos de las manos y diez deditos de los pies / Ten Little Fingers and Ten Little Toes by Mem Fox, illustrated by Helen Oxenbury, translated by F. Isabel Campoy
   ❯ This bilingual board book counts the fingers and toes of babies all over the world.

La piñata / The Piñata by Rita Rosa Ruesga, illustrated by Soledad Sebastián
   ❯ A collection of bilingual songs with musical notations.

Relevant Websites

Brooklyn Public Library: Ready Set Kindergarten! Hablando / Talk
www.bklynlibrary.org/first-5-years/ready-set-kindergarten-espa%C3% B1ol-hablando-talking-spanish
   ❯ This video for parents about the importance of talking with babies includes lots of ideas for activities to do at home. An English-language companion to this resource is also available.

King County Library System: Tell Me a Story / Saco una manita
http://tmas.kcls.org/spanish-saco-una-manita/
   ❯ A fantastic video demonstration of this traditional children's song.

PROGRAM TITLE	DEVELOPED BY	THEME
Animalitos / Little Critters	Katie Scherrer	Dogs / Perros

Opening Routine

Sing in English and Spanish to the tune of "Where Is Thumbkin?" Change the song to "Buenas tardes / Good Afternoon" or "Buenas noches / Good Evening" to match the time of your program.

Buenos días	Good Morning
Buenos días. Buenos días.	Good morning. Good morning.
¿Cómo estás? ¿Cómo estás?	How are you? How are you?
Muy bien, gracias. Muy bien, gracias.	Very well, thank you. Very well, thank you.
¿Y tú? ¿Y tú?	And you? And you?

Song

"Un amigo me enseñó" from *Buenos días Babyradio: Música infantil* by
   Babyradio (CD)
   ❯ This song introduces various animals and their sounds. Consider making
   flannelboard pieces or using puppets to go along with the song.

Book

Ten Little Puppies / Diez perritos by Alma Flor Ada and F. Isabel Campoy, illustrated by Ulises Wensell, English translation by Rosalma Zibizarreta
   ❯ This bilingual book, adapted from a traditional nursery rhyme in Spanish,
   counts down a group of puppies from ten to one. Musical notation for the song
   is included.

Traditional Song

After reading the book, sing the song!

Diez perritos

Yo tenía diez perritos,
yo tenía diez perritos.
Uno se perdió en la nieve.
No me quedan más que nueve.

De los nueve que quedaban,
de los nueve que quedaban,
uno se comió un bizcocho.
No me quedan más que ocho.

De los ocho que quedaban,
de los ocho que quedaban
uno se metió en un brete.
No me quedan más que siete.

De los siete que quedaron,
de los siete que quedaron,
uno ya no le veréis.
No me quedan más que seis.

De los seis que me quedaron
de los seis que me quedaron,
uno se mató de un brinco.
No me quedan más que cinco.

De los cinco que quedaron,
de los cinco que quedaron,
uno se mató en el teatro.
No me quedan más que cuatro.

De los cuatro que quedaban,
de los cuatro que quedaban,
uno se volvió al revés.
No me quedan más que tres.

De los tres que me quedaban,
de los tres que me quedaban,
uno se murió de tos.
No me quedan más que dos.

De los dos que me quedaban,
de los dos que me quedaban,
uno se volvió un tuno.
No me queda más que uno.

Y el que me quedaba
un día se marchó al campo
y ya no me queda ninguno
de los diez perritos.

Book

¡Perros! ¡Perros! Dogs! Dogs! by Ginger Foglesong Guy, illustrated by Sharon
    Glick
    ❯ Very simple bilingual text uses lots of dogs to introduce adjectives and
    opposites.

Traditional Song

Sing this song a few times, changing the "Bark! Bark!" to other movements each time. For example, try "Clap! Clap!," "Stomp! Stomp!," and "Jump! Jump!"

How Much Is That Doggie in the Window?

How much is that doggie in the window? (Bark! Bark!)
The one with the waggly tail.
How much is that doggie in the window? (Bark! Bark!)
I do hope that doggie's for sale!

Closing Routine

Sing to the tune of "Where Is Thumbkin?"

Canción de despedida	Goodbye Song
Adiós amigos. Adiós amigos.	Goodbye friends. Goodbye friends.
Ya me voy. Ya me voy.	It's time to go. It's time to go.
Me dio mucho gusto, estar con ustedes.	I had lots of fun at storytime today.
Adiós. Adiós.	Goodbye. Goodbye.

Extension Activity

Doggie Opposites

INSTRUCTIONS

Print images of lots of dogs that match the phrases used in ¡*Perros! ¡Perros! Dogs! Dogs!* Also print or write on index cards the various descriptions used in the book, such as "perro grande / big dog" and "perro chico / little dog." Encourage adults to help children find dogs that match the various descriptions. Talk about the various pairs of opposites and what makes the dogs similar and different.

MATERIALS NEEDED

- Printed pictures of various dogs
- Bilingual word pairs

Bonus Storytime Resources

"El perro dice" from *Mis amigos los animales* by Mona Warner (CD)
> ❯ Learn animal names and their sounds in Spanish as you sing along to this song.

Un gato y un perro / A Cat and a Dog by Claire Masurel, illustrated by Bob Kolar, translated by Andrés Antreasyan
> ❯ A cat and a dog are definitely not friends, until they realize that maybe they can help each other.

Relevant Websites

GuíaInfantil: Diez perritos
www.guiainfantil.com/videos/canciones-infantiles/cancion-infantil
-diez-perritos/
> ❯ An animated video of this traditional song led by the GuíaInfantil mascot, Oso Traposo.

Making Learning Fun: Felt Board for Dog's Colorful Day
www.makinglearningfun.com/themepages/DogsFeltBoard.htm
> ❯ Flannelboard pattern for this popular story by Emma Dodd.

YouTube: Babyradio—"Un amigo me enseñó"
www.youtube.com/watch?v=iA3RB_Ujsvs
> ❯ A cute, animated video to accompany this song.

AGE
RANGE
Toddlers

PROGRAM TITLE	DEVELOPED BY	THEME
Peekaboo Stories! / ¡Cucú cuentos!	Katie Scherrer	Frogs / Las ranas

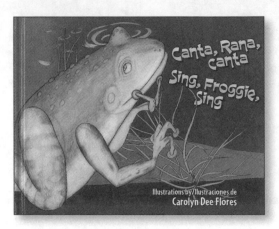

Opening Routine

You can sing this bilingual song to the tune of "Frère Jacques" in a variety of ways. First try singing it as a call and response song in Spanish. Then do the same in English, and then bilingually.

Hola niños	Hello children
Hola niños.	Hello children.
¿Cómo están?	How are you?
Muy bien, gracias.	Very well, thank you.
¿Y tú?	How about you?

Traditional Song

This is a fun, silly children's song known by many in Latin America. There are many different versions with slightly different lyrics. Sing in Spanish only or in both languages. To make more interactive, have the group hop like frogs each time you repeat "cucú."

Cucú, cucú cantaba la rana	Cucú, cucú the Little Frog Sings
Cucú, cucú cantaba la rana.	Cucú, cucú the little frog sings.
Cucú, cucú debajo del agua.	Cucú, cucú while watching many things.
Cucú, cucú pasó un caballero.	Cucú, cucú like the man who sat.
Cucú, cucú con capa y sombrero.	Cucú, cucú wearing a coat and hat.
Cucú, cucú pasó una señora.	Cucú, cucú a lady came along.
Cucú, cucú con traje de cola.	Cucú, cucú wearing a dress so long.
Cucú, cucú pasó un marinero.	Cucú, cucú there's a sailor so merry.
Cucú, cucú vendiendo romero.	Cucú, cucú who is selling rosemary.
Cucú, cucú le pidió un ramito.	Cucú, cucú the frog asked to buy some.
Cucú, cucú no le quiso dar.	Cucú, cucú but he passed her by.
Cucú, cucú y se echó a llorar.	Cucú, cucú so she started to cry.

Book

Wiggling Pockets / Los bolsillos saltarines by Pat Mora, illustrated by
Maribel Suárez
   ❶ Danny has a surprise—a frog! It jumps throughout the house, bringing giggles to everyone in the family along the way.

Flannelboard

Continue using Spanish as you share this traditional English-language rhyme by counting the frogs in both languages after each verse.

Five Green and Speckled Frogs

Five green and speckled frogs
Sat on a speckled log
Eating some most delicious bugs.
One jumped into the pool
Where it was nice and cool.
Now there are four green speckled frogs.

Continue with song, removing one frog at a time until the last verse.

One green and speckled frog
Sat on a speckled log
Eating some most delicious bugs.
She jumped into the pool
Where it was nice and cool.
Now there are no green speckled frogs.

Book

Jump, Frog, Jump! by Robert Kalan, illustrated by Byron Barton; translated by
Aída E. Marcuse as *¡Salta, ranita, salta!*
❯ This classic cumulative tale of a frog who escapes danger by jumping can be
made more interactive with the use of frog stick puppets or simple movements
for each of the animals mentioned in the story. If reading in one language,
choose key vocabulary (such as the names of the various animals) to repeat
in the second language as you read.

Traditional Rhyme

This rhyme is often told by adults to comfort children when they have a small
injury. Say the rhyme several times, having children find various parts of their
body each time. This is a great opportunity for children and adult caregivers to
snuggle up together . . . maybe even add a little tickle at the end!

Sana, sana colita de rana

Sana, sana
colita de rana
si no sanas hoy
sanarás mañana.

Closing Routine

"Adiós, amigos" from *Ole! Ole! Ole! Dr. Jean en Español* by Jean Feldman (CD)

Extension Activity

Frog Sizes

INSTRUCTIONS

Adults and children can work together to put the frogs in order from small to large. Give children a stack of five paper frogs. Encourage adults to help the children organize the frogs from smallest to largest and then glue them to a piece of paper, perhaps drawing a log for the frogs to sit on as well. Practice counting in English and Spanish.

MATERIALS NEEDED

- Precut frogs of various sizes
- Blank paper
- Drawing supplies for detailing
- Glue sticks

Bonus Storytime Resources

Canta, Rana, canta / Sing, Froggie, Sing by Natalia Rosales-Yeomans, illustrated by Carolyn Dee Flores
    ❯ A bilingual, picture book version of a traditional children's song known widely throughout the Spanish-speaking world.

Hop, Jump by Ellen Stoll Walsh; translated by Alma Flor Ada and F. Isabel Campoy as *Salta y brinca*
    ❯ In a world where everyone hops and jumps, one little froggie longs to dance.

Relevant Websites

GuíaInfantil: "Cucú, cantaba la rana"
www.guiainfantil.com/videos/canciones-infantiles/cu-cu-cantaba-la-rana
    -cancion-infantil/
    ❯ A cute music video led by the GuíaInfantil mascot, Oso Traposo.

StoryPlace: "Coloree el arcoiris"
www.storyplace.org/es/cuento/coloree-el-arcoiris
    ❯ Freda the frog introduces the colors of the rainbow in this online story from Charlotte Mecklenburg Library.

AGE RANGE
Toddlers

PROGRAM TITLE	DEVELOPED BY	THEME
Bilingüitos	Kelly Von Zee	Palabras por todas partes / Words Everywhere

Opening Routine

Sing to the tune of "The Bear Went Over the Mountain," inserting the name of each child to welcome everyone to storytime.

La canción de nombres

Hello _____,
hola _____,
hello _____,
y bienvenido(a)!

Traditional Rhyme

Clap as you sing the various syllables that make up the word *cho-co-la-te*. While singing the final line, pretend to stir the chocolate, and then touch your nose.

Chocolate

¡Uno, dos, tres, CHO!
¡Uno, dos, tres, CO!
¡Uno, dos, tres, LA!
¡Uno, dos, tres, TE!
Bate, bate, chocolate, tu nariz de cacahuate.

Book

Quinito's Neighborhood / El vecindario de Quinito by Ina Cumpiano, illustrated by
  José Ramírez
    ❯ Join Quinito as he goes on a trip through his neighborhood, noting the
    diverse occupations of the people he encounters along the way.

Movement Song

"Los niños cuando bailan" from ¡*A Bailar! Let's Dance! Spanish Learning Songs*
  by Jorge Anaya (CD)
    ❯ Find the various parts of the body as you dance and sing to this fun version
    of a traditional song.

Book

Opuestos: Mexican Folk Art Opposites in English and Spanish by Cynthia Weill,
  artwork by Quirino and Martín Santiago
    ❯ Explore pairs of opposites and photographs of beautiful artwork from
    Mexico.

Game

Simón dice / Simon Says
Ask the kids to point to various body parts and engage in simple movements
(such as jump, clap, etc.)—for example, ¡Simón dice . . . salta! ¡Simón dice . . .
que toques la nariz!

Closing Routine

"Adiós, amigos" from *Diez Deditos: Ten Little Fingers and Other Play Rhymes and
Action Songs from Latin America* by José-Luis Orozco (CD)

Extension Activity

Rhyming Game / El juego de las rimas

Make your own set of rhyming word cards in Spanish. Encourage the adults to work with the children to find and match the rhyming words. A list of suggested Spanish rhyming words follows. A free printable sheet of Spanish rhyming word cards is also available from Spanish Playground at www.spanishplayground .net/wp-content/uploads/2012/09/rimar-tarjetas.pdf.

estrella/botella	aguja/bruja	anillo/martillo	ratón/corazón	toro/loro
pan/flan	sol/caracol	conejo/espejo	botón/león	cuna/luna
rana/lana	ventana/campana	gato/pato	elefante/volante	niña/piña

Bonus Storytime Resources

Nicomedes el pelón by Pinto and Chinto
> ❯ In this fun Spanish book, a man goes bald and then puts all kinds of funny things on his head to cover his baldness, but nothing works.

Uno, Dos, Tres: My First Spanish Rhymes by Yanitzia Canetti, illustrated by Patrice Aggs
> ❯ This wonderful collection of Spanish nursery rhymes includes an audio CD.

Relevant Websites

¡Es divertido hablar dos idiomas!: Picky Paul
http://bilingualchildrensprogramming.blogspot.com/2013/07/flannel-friday -giveaway-picky-paul.html
> ❯ A flannelboard pattern and bilingual storytelling instructions are included for this cute story about a picky eater that introduces vocabulary of various foods. Based on a story in *Mudluscious: Stories and Activities Featuring Food for Preschool Children* by Jan Irving and Robin Currie.

StoryBlocks: Chocolate, Chocolate
www.storyblocks.org/videos/chocolate-chocolate/
> ❯ A demonstration of this traditional rhyme, including instructions and early literacy tips.

PROGRAM TITLE	DEVELOPED BY	THEME
¡Cantos! ¡Cuentos! ¡Juegos! / Songs! Stories! Games!	Katie Scherrer	Party / La fiesta

AGE RANGE
Preschoolers

Opening Routine

"Estamos contentos" from *Escucha y disfruta con Mama Gansa / Listen, Like, Learn with Mother Goose on the Loose en Español* by Evelio Mendez Rahel and Betsy Diamant-Cohen (CD)

 ❍ English and Spanish versions of this simple greeting song are available on this CD.

Book

Book Fiesta! Celebrate Children's Day, Book Day / Celebremos El día de los niños, El día de los libros by Pat Mora, illustrated by Rafael López

 ❍ You don't have to wait for El día de los niños / Children's Day (April 30) to share this joyful bilingual book that celebrates books and reading. Any day is a great day for a book fiesta!

Movement Song

"El baile de las manos" from *¡A bailar! / Let's Dance!* by Jorge Anaya (CD)

 ❍ Move your hands in the following ways as you dance and sing.

arriba / up	a los lados / to the sides	adelante / in front
abajo / down	aplaudir / clapping	atrás / behind

Book

Dale, dale, dale: Una fiesta de números / Hit It, Hit It, Hit It: A Fiesta of Numbers by
   René Saldaña Jr., illustrated by Carolyn Dee Flores
   ❷ This bilingual birthday celebration incorporates counting and introduces
   a traditional Mexican song that is sung when children try to hit the piñata.

Traditional Song

This song is often sung at parties in Mexico when children break the piñata.
There are several versions with slightly different lyrics. This version does not
translate the words literally from Spanish to English but instead maintains a
similar rhythm and rhyme.

Dale, dale, dale	Hit It, Hit It, Hit It
Dale, dale, dale.	Hit it, hit it, hit it.
No pierdas el tino.	But don't lose your aim!
Porque si lo pierdes,	Close your eyes and try it.
pierdes el camino.	Play the piñata game!
Ya le diste una.	You try to hit it one time.
Ya le diste dos.	You take a second turn.
Ya le diste tres.	You try it for a third time.
Y su tiempo se acabó.	Now it's another friend's turn.

Flannelboard

Stuff the Piñata!

You may not be able to break a real piñata in the library, but you can create a
flannelboard version. Place the empty "piñata" on the flannelboard and invite
children to come up one at a time to help you put small items inside it, such as
cars, rings, and candies. Don't forget to add lots of confetti! A sample flannelboard pattern can be found at http://bilingualchildrensprogramming.blogspot
.com/2012/09/bilingual-storytime-la-pinata.html.
   After you stuff the flannel piñata, invite the children to close their eyes and
count uno, dos, tres. Then surprise them by revealing a real piñata. Use lots of
words to describe the piñata in Spanish and English. You may want to provide
each child with a small toy or candy if you are not able to break the piñata
together as a group.

Closing Routine

"Candombe de las despedidas" from *Canticuénticos Embrujados* by
Canticuénticos (CD)
> ● This Uruguayan-style song (from the Argentine children's group Canticuén-
ticos) is long enough to use for an extended goodbye routine, such as blowing
bubbles, stamping hands, or passing out stickers.

Extension Activity

Piñata Confetti Math

Children sort piñata confetti by various attributes such as color, shape, and size.

INSTRUCTIONS

Make piñata confetti by cutting paper shapes of various sizes and colors. Encourage adults to help children sort the confetti by its various attributes. Adults can
also help children count the confetti and practice making patterns. Find bilingual instructions for this activity for parents and caregivers at http://tinyurl
.com/pinatamath.

MATERIALS NEEDED

• Precut shapes of various sizes and colors to serve as piñata confetti.

Bonus Storytime Resources

Marisol McDonald and the Clash Bash / Marisol McDonald y la fiesta sin igual
by Monica Brown, illustrated by Sara Palacios, translated by Adriana
Domínguez
> ● Marisol struggles to pick just one theme for her birthday party when she
enjoys so many different things. A longer title, this book may be best read in
one language, incorporating key vocabulary from the other language along
the way.

"¡Dale, dale, dale!" from *¡Cantemos en Español!* by Fisher-Price (CD)
> ● This is an upbeat version of the traditional song.

¡Fiesta! by Ginger Foglesong Guy, illustrated by René King Moreno
> ● This simple bilingual counting book introduces the various trinkets that
go inside a piñata.

Relevant Websites

Bandcamp: Canticuénticos—"Candombe de las despedidas"
https://canticuenticos.bandcamp.com/track/candombe-de-las-despedidas
> ❯ Here you can stream the song, read the lyrics, and find information about this group.

Pat Mora: *Book Fiesta!*
www.patmora.com/ideas/#bookfiesta
> ❯ Ideas for teachers and librarians for sharing this special book with children.

Whistlefritz: ¡*A bailar! / Let's Dance!* Translation Guide
www.whistlefritz.com/wp-content/uploads/2015/02/bailar-booklet-download.pdf
> ❯ Find lyrics and key vocabulary translations for the songs on this CD.

AGE
RANGE
Preschoolers

PROGRAM TITLE	DEVELOPED BY	THEME
¡Cuéntame Cuentos! Storytime!	Katie Scherrer and Jamie Campbell Naidoo	La granja / Farm

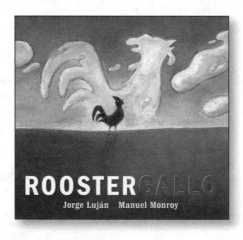
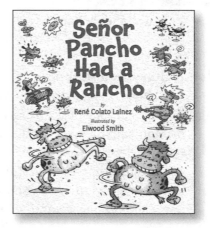

Opening Routine

"Hola amigo" from *Ole! Ole! Ole! Dr. Jean en Español* by Dr. Jean Feldman (CD)

Book

Señor Pancho Had a Rancho by René Colato Laínez, illustrated by Elwood Smith
> ❯ Spanish-speaking and English-speaking farm animals learn new words and dance across the barnyard in this joyful book that blends English and Spanish onomatopoeia and invites readers to sing along.

Bilingual Song

"Mi granja (My Farm)" from *Piñata and More: Bilingual Songs for Children* by
  Sarah Barchas (CD)
  ● Meet the various animals that live on the farm in Spanish and English in
  this bilingual version of a traditional children's song. Make this song more
  interactive with puppets or simple animal-inspired movements.

Book

¡No, Tito, no! / No, No Titus! by Claire Masurel, illustrated by Shari Halpern,
  translated by Diego Lasconi
  ● Tito (Titus) is a new puppy on the farm. He must learn what all the animals
  who live on the farm do in order to learn his own role and be a good dog.

Traditional Song

This traditional children's song provides a perfect opportunity for children and
their adult caregivers to snuggle up together. Sing in Spanish and English.

Los pollitos	The Little Chicks
Los pollitos dicen	All the little chicks say
pío, pío, pío	Peep, peep, peep
cuando tienen hambre	When they are hungry
cuando tienen frío.	And when they're too cold to sleep.
La gallina busca	The mother hen goes looking
el maíz y el trigo.	For some corn and wheat.
Les da la comida	She keeps the little chicks warm,
y les presta abrigo.	She gives them food to eat.
Bajo sus dos alas	Snuggled up together
acurrucaditos	Underneath her wings
hasta el otro día	Until the morning comes
duermen los pollitos.	The little chicks all sleep.

Book

Rooster / Gallo by Jorge Luján, illustrated by Manuel Monroy, translated by
Elisa Amado
> ❯ In this bilingual poem, the rooster wakes up the world with his canción—
his song.

Closing Routine

"Adiós, amigos" from *Diez Deditos: Ten Little Fingers and Other Play Rhymes and
Action Songs from Latin America* by José-Luis Orozco (CD)

Extension Activity

Animal Sort

INSTRUCTIONS

Children can practice sorting by working with a small group of animal toys or
pictures. They can sort the animals that live on a farm from those that live else-
where (desert, jungle, ocean, etc.) and place the farm animals with the barn. If
you are using pictures, children can glue the farm animals to the picture of their
barn. Encourage adults to work with their child and talk about the animals that
live on the farm. They could make up a story about what would happen if a new
animal, such as a lion or an elephant, moved to the farm!

MATERIALS NEEDED

- Pictures of barns or a toy barn
- Pictures of various animals or various animal toys
- Glue sticks (if gluing pictures of animals to the picture of a barn)
- Crayons for detailing farm (optional)

Bonus Storytime Resources

How Big Is a Pig? by Clare Beaton, illustrated by Stella Blackstone; translated
by Yanitzia Canetti as *Cerdota grandota*
> ❯ Through rhyming text (in both English and Spanish versions) and unique
mixed-media illustrations, this fun story introduces farm animals and opposites as we try to find out how big a pig is.

Why Are You Doing That? by Elisa Amado, illustrated by Manuel Monroy
> ❯ A little boy in a rural area visits his farming neighbors in order to learn about
the many steps involved in growing and harvesting food. Spanish words are
blended seamlessly into the predominantly English text.

Digital Learning Extensions

Los Pollitos digital app by Cantos
https://itunes.apple.com/us/app/los-pollitos/id527097576?mt=8
> ❯ This musical app teaches children the popular Latin American song "Los pollitos." Functionality includes multiple options for singers in English and Spanish. Hot spots encourage children to prompt each chick to sing "pío, pío, pío" as well as facilitate interactions between the mother hen and her chicks. Children and caregivers can share the app together on individual digital tablets during storytime, or the storytime facilitator can display the app on the overhead screen to model functionality, encouraging children to come up and interact with the app. Children can demonstrate how the hen feeds her young and sing along, too.

Felt Board digital app by Software Smoothie
https://itunes.apple.com/us/app/felt-board/id492342753?mt=8
> ❯ Resembling an actual feltboard with felt storytelling pieces, this creative app has a multitude of uses during bilingual storytime. For this particular program, children can use the app to retell any of the books shared during storytime or tell their own farm-related story using the feltboard pieces. The storytime facilitator can display the app on the overhead screen and invite children to help move the storytelling pieces. Alternatively, digital tablets can be distributed to allow children and caregivers to explore the app together.

Relevant Websites

Holiday House: *Señor Pancho Had a Rancho* Farm Animal Sound Match
www.holidayhouse.com/docs/SenorPancho_2014.pdf
> ❯ Match the animals (in Spanish) with their sounds (in English).

StoryBlocks: "Los pollitos dicen"
www.storyblocks.org/project/los-pollitos-dicen/
> ❯ A video of this traditional song sung in Spanish.

PROGRAM TITLE	DEVELOPED BY	THEME
Rima, rima / Spanish Rhyme Time	Kacy Vega	Rhymes / Las rimas

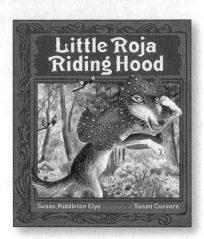

Opening Routine

"Buenos días amiguitos" from *¡Sabor! Spanish Learning Songs* by Jorge Anaya
(CD)
> ◉ Greet the day using lots of weather vocabulary such as lluvioso (rainy), frío
> (cold), and cálido (hot).

Book

María tenía una llamita / Maria Had a Little Llama by Angela Dominguez
> ◉ This delightful, bilingual rendition of a popular children's rhyme is set in
> the Peruvian countryside.

Song

"Rimas 1" from *Sal y pimiento* by Susy Dorn (CD)
> ◉ Listen for and review the Spanish words that rhyme in this silly song about
> animals who play musical instruments. Make this song more interactive by
> creating feltboard pieces or incorporating real instrument play.

Book

Little Roja Riding Hood by Susan Middleton Elya, illustrated by Susan Guevara
> ◉ This fresh take on the Little Red Riding Hood story includes Spanish words
> interspersed throughout the rhyming English text.

Traditional Rhyme

Clap along to the rhythm as you share this rhyme.

Aserrín, aserrán

Aserrín, aserrán
los maderos de San Juan.
Piden pan no les dan,
piden huesos y les dan queso.

Book

¡Muu, Moo! Rimas de animales / Animal Nursery Rhymes by Alma Flor Ada and F. Isabel Campoy, illustrated by Viví Escrivá; English translation by Rosalma Zubizarreta
  ◉ Select a few nursery rhymes to recite in Spanish or English, or both!

Closing Routine

The *colorín colorado* saying is a popular way to close a story in Spanish-speaking countries. This English translation is not literal, but it invokes a similar spirit and maintains the rhyme.

Colorín colorado, este cuento se ha acabado!	It's time my friend for our stories to end!

Extension Activity

Rhyme Time! ¡A rimar!

INSTRUCTIONS

This activity can be done together as a group or in small groups or pairs with adult caregivers playing together with their child(ren). A beanbag or soft ball is passed between child and adult. The adult selects a pair of rhyming words and says, "Yo digo / I say _____, tú dices / you say _____" and then rolls the ball to the child. The child may need to hear the rhyme and the word repeated a few times. The child then rolls the ball back to the adult, and the adult initiates a new rhyme. Encourage adults to share rhymes they remember from their own childhood. This activity can be done in both English and Spanish, depending on the group. Here are a few two-syllable rhyming words in Spanish to get you started.

Adult	Child
gato (cat)	pato (duck)
río (river)	frío (cold)
luna (moon)	cuna (baby's crib)
cosa (thing)	rosa (rose)
beso (kiss)	peso (Mexican money)
queso (cheese)	hueso (bone)
casa (house)	taza (cup)
pito (whistle)	frito (fried)

MATERIALS NEEDED

- Small beanbags or soft balls. The amount needed will depend on the size of the group and whether you plan to do the activity together as a group or in pairs of adult caregivers and children.

Bonus Storytime Resources

The Moon Is La Luna: Silly Rhymes in English and Spanish by Jay Harris, illustrated by Matthew Cordell
  ❯ This book is full of short rhymes in English that incorporate Spanish words.

"Aserrín, aserrán" from *Coloreando: Traditional Songs for Children in Spanish* by Marta Gómez (CD)
  ❯ This is a soft, simple version of the traditional song.

Mamá Goose: Un Tesoro de rimas infantiles / A Latino Nursery Treasury by Alma Flor Ada and F. Isabel Campoy, illustrated by Maribel Suárez
  ❯ An extensive collection of rhymes, riddles, and games from the Spanish-speaking world paired with wonderful English translations.

Relevant Websites

King County Library System: Tell Me a Story—Rhymes and Songs
http://tmas.kcls.org/category/rhymes_songs/
  ❯ A massive online collection of songs and rhymes for children, including many rhymes in languages other than English. In addition to words and lyrics, most include a video demonstration.

Mama Lisa's World
www.mamalisa.com/
> An extensive collection of children's rhymes from around the world, available in multiple languages.

Paka Paka: Audios
www.pakapaka.gob.ar/audios/
> Paka Paka is an educational television channel for children and families operated by Argentina's Ministry of Education. This site provides Spanish-language audio content that families can enjoy together, including songs, stories, and tongue twisters.

PROGRAM TITLE	DEVELOPED BY	THEME
What Grows in Your Garden? / **¿Qué hay en tu jardín?**	Kacy Vega	Nature / La naturaleza

AGE RANGE
Preschoolers

Opening Routine

"H-E-L-L-O" from *From Here to There* by Nathalia Palis (CD)
> This fun bilingual song greets children and teaches them to spell both "Hello" and "Hola" while they sing and dance.

Book

Grandpa Green by Lane Smith; translated by Paulina de Aguinaco Martin as *El jardín del abuelo*
> A little boy learns about his great grandfather's personal history as he walks through the elderly man's topiary garden.

Movement Song

"La Semilla" from *Spanish All Year Round* by Spanish Together (CD)
> ⦿ Show children how to imitate a growing seed while singing this song. Crouch down and then slowly rise, lifting and outstretching arms to represent the growth of a plant or flower.

Book

Amo nuestra tierra / I Love Our Earth by Bill Martin Jr. and Michael Sampson, photographs by Dan Lipow, translated by Yanitzia Canetti
> ⦿ Celebrate the diversity of our earth with this brief, bilingual book that is illustrated with beautiful photos of real people and real landscapes from around the world.

Movement Song

"Llueve" from *Play in Spanish* by Spanish Together (CD)
> ⦿ Two key action words in this song are llueve (rain) and corre (run). For *llueve*, encourage kids to imitate the rain by wiggling all their fingers in the air while slowly lowering them. When the verse switches to *corre*, model how to run in place.

Book

Call Me Tree / Llámame árbol by Maya Christina Gonzalez, translated by Dana Goldberg
> ⦿ A child grows from a seed into a strong tree, one of many in a forest of diverse children, in this beautiful book that encourages movement and self-esteem.

Closing Routine

"Adiós" from *Play in Spanish* by Spanish Together (CD)

Extension Activity

Use *Grandpa Green / El jardín del abuelo* as inspiration to talk about family history. Encourage children and adult caregivers to have conversations about grandparents. Does your grandpa or grandma have any special talents like Grandpa Green? ¿Qué es especial de sus abuelos?

Bonus Storytime Resources

"Que llueva" from *Cha Cha Cha: Spanish Learning Songs* by Jorge Anaya (CD)
> ❯ A traditional Latin American children's song about the rain.

My Garden / Mi jardín by Rebecca Emberley
> ❯ Simple pictures display items associated with gardening. Items are labeled in English and Spanish.

Gathering the Sun: An Alphabet in Spanish and English by Alma Flor Ada, illustrated by Rosalma Zubizarreta, English translation by Rosalma Zubizarreta
> ❯ Short, bilingual poems explore the natural world from A to Z.

Relevant Websites

GuíaInfantil: "Que llueva"
www.guiainfantil.com/servicios/musica/Canciones/que_llueva.htm
> ❯ Lyrics and a video for this traditional song.

Los niños en su casa: Un cartel de naturaleza
www.losninosensucasa.org/activity.php?id=35
> ❯ Spanish instructions for making a nature poster. Also available in English at www.aplaceofourown.org/activity.php?id=35.

Spanish Playground: Take a Spanish Nature Walk
www.spanishplayground.net/spanish-nature-walk/
> ❯ Instructions for taking a nature walk with a link to a printable checklist of Spanish vocabulary for items you may encounter along the way.

AGE RANGE
Preschoolers

PROGRAM TITLE	DEVELOPED BY	THEME
Under the Sea / Bajo el mar	Kacy Vega	Water / El agua

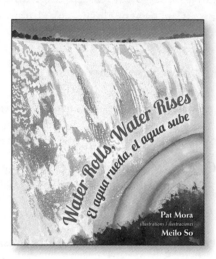

Opening Routine

"Yo me llamo" from *Baile y canto* by Maria Fernanda y Sus Amigos (CD)
> As you dance together to the music, call on volunteers to shout out their own names.

Book

Bajo las olas 1, 2, 3 / Under the Sea 1, 2, 3 by Barbara Knox, translated by Martin Luis Guzman Ferrer
> Count in English and Spanish as you explore various forms of marine life.

Bilingual Song

Sing this bilingual song to the tune of "The Wheels on the Bus." Include movements for each animal to increase the interactivity.

Los tiburones en la mar	The Sharks in the Sea
Los tiburones en la mar hacen chomp, chomp, chomp	The sharks in the sea go chomp, chomp, chomp
chomp, chomp, chomp,	Chomp, chomp, chomp,
chomp, chomp, chomp.	Chomp, chomp, chomp.
Los tiburones en la mar hacen chomp, chomp, chomp	The sharks in the sea go chomp, chomp, chomp
todo el día.	All day long.
Las langostas en la mar hacen pinch, pinch, pinch . . .	The lobsters in the sea go pinch, pinch, pinch . . .
La ballena en la mar hace squirt, squirt, squirt . . .	The whale in the sea goes squirt, squirt, squirt . . .
Las almejas en la mar se abren y se cierran . . .	The clams in the sea go open and shut . . .
El pulpo en la mar se menea, se menea, se menea . . .	The octopus in the sea goes wiggle, wiggle, wiggle . . .
El caballo de mar va adelante y atrás . . .	The seahorse in the sea rocks back and forth . . .
Los niños en la mar saltan arriba y abajo . . .	The kids in the waves jump up and down . . .

Book

I Know the River Loves Me / Yo sé que el río me ama by Maya Christina Gonzalez
   ❥ A young girl watches the river change throughout the year. She expresses the ways in which she knows the river loves her and how she in turn cares for the river.

Spanish Song

"Elena la ballena" from *Mis amigos los animales* by Mona Warner (CD)
   ❥ This is a fun, upbeat version of this traditional song about a whale who lives in the ocean. Try to keep up as the song gets faster and faster!

Book

Water Rolls, Water Rises / El agua rueda, el agua sube by Pat Mora, illustrated by
Meilo So, translated by Adriana Domínguez
- ◉ Gentle poems present water in various landscapes around the world.

Closing Routine

"Adiós" from *Baile y canto* by Maria Fernanda y Sus Amigos (CD)

Extension Activity

Sea Creature Sculptures

INSTRUCTIONS

Review some of the sea life mentioned during the storytime. Encourage children to mold different sea creatures out of Play-Doh. Make sure to model for all ages and offer supports for young children who are still developing fine motor skills. Post visuals of various sea creature shapes to help the young sculptors. Simple creations might include a whale tail or a starfish. If you have seashells, incorporate those, too, and let children make impressions in the Play-Doh using the shells. To set the ocean ambience, play soft music in the background that resembles ocean waves or singing whales.

MATERIALS NEEDED

- One regular can of Play-Doh per child
- Table with hard surface
- Objects, such as seashells, to make impressions; seashells can be purchased in bulk from companies such as Oriental Trading (www.orientaltrading .com)
- Paper towels or wipes for cleaning up

Bonus Storytime Resources

Hello Ocean / Hola mar by Pam Muñoz Ryan, illustrated by Mark Astrella, translated by Yanitzia Canetti
- ◉ A young child discovers the ocean through her five senses.

"La vibora" from *¡Fantástico!* by Lucky Diaz and the Family Jam Band (CD)
- ◉ Lucky Diaz and the Family Jam Band present a modern version of a traditional song about an ocean snake. This song is also a popular children's game.

Relevant Websites

¡Es divertido hablar dos idiomas!: "Los tiburones en la mar"
http://bilingualchildrensprogramming.blogspot.com/2012/05/bilingual
-storytime-flannel-friday-los.html
> A blog post with a flannelboard pattern to accompany this song.

Pat Mora: *Water Rolls, Water Rises* Classroom Guide
www.patmora.com/images/water-rolls-teachers-guide.pdf
> Extensive collection of activities and other ideas for engaging students around this book.

PROGRAM TITLE	DEVELOPED BY	THEME
Tiempo de cuentos / Storytime	Adriana Silva	Food / La comida

AGE RANGE
Preschoolers

Opening Routine

Have a boy puppet on hand when families are arriving for storytime. Introduce the puppet as "Pin Pon" and encourage each child to shake his hand.

Once you're sitting down in the storytime circle, ask the children what they did to get ready in the morning. Tell them that Pin Pon (who is sitting on your lap) washed his face and brushed his hair. Sing "Pin Pon," a traditional Spanish children's song about a little boy doll.

Pin Pon

Pin Pon es un muñeco muy guapo de cartón.
Se lava la carita con agua y con jabón.
Se desenreda el pelo con peine de marfil.
Y aunque se da tirones no llora ni hace así: "buuuuu"
Pin Pon dame la mano, con un buen apretón.
Que quiero ser tu amigo . . . Pin Pon . . . Pin Pon . . . Pin Pon . . .

Book

Green Is a Chile Pepper by Roseanne Greenfield Thong, illustrated by John Parra
- Explore a colorful world of Latino foods in this book that blends Spanish words into the rhyming English text.

Music Activity

"El frutero" from *Cha, Cha, Cha, Spanish Learning Songs* by Jorge Anaya (CD)
- Dance and sing along to this song using egg shakers or fruit props that match the fruits mentioned in the song.

peras / pears	uvas / grapes	manzanas / apples	sandías / watermelon
frambuesas / raspberries	fresas / strawberries	cerezas / cherries	melones / melons
piñas / pineapples	limones / lemons	bananas / bananas	frutas / fruits

Book

Salsa: Un poema para cocinar / Salsa: A Cooking Poem by Jorge Argueta, illustrated by Duncan Tonatiuh, translated by Elisa Amado
- A brother and sister make a delicious salsa, singing and dancing along the way as they imagine the various ingredients are instruments in an orchestra.

Flannelboard Activity

Make a pizza! Start with three large, flannel circles: the tan pizza base, red tomato sauce, and yellow cheese. Make the circles by inverting three nesting mixing bowls onto the colored felts and tracing around the bowls. Stack the cutout circles with just the edges showing each layer. Give the children various toppings to add to the pizza one at a time while reviewing the vocabulary in Spanish and English, such as tomatoes/tomates, mushrooms/setas, and olives/aceitunas. An example of a flannelboard pizza can be found on the *Storytime Katie* blog at http://storytimekatie.com/2011/04/15/flannel-friday-pizza/.

Book

Let's Eat! / ¡A comer! by Pat Mora, illustrated by Maribel Suárez
> ❯ A family sits down together for a healthy dinner, grateful for their many joys. Very short sentences in English and Spanish make this book an ideal bilingual read-aloud.

Closing Routine

"Adiós" from ¡*Sabor! Spanish Learning Songs* by Jorge Anaya (CD)
> ❯ Take the Pin Pon puppet around the group, shaking children's hands to say goodbye.

Extension Activity

Pretend Play: The Restaurant

INSTRUCTIONS

Cut out pictures of various foods from grocery ads and magazines. Go over the vocabulary in English and Spanish. Let children make a menu by pasting the pictures onto a folder or piece of paper. Encourage the children and their caregivers to name their restaurant and, with the adults' help, write the name on the front. Do the children recognize any letters? Name those they do not know. Have more paper on hand so that the "server" can write down orders.

MATERIALS NEEDED

- Various food pictures
- Folders or paper (can be construction paper)
- Markers, crayons, or colored pencils
- Glue sticks

Bonus Storytime Resources

"Chocolate" from *Baile y canto* by Maria Fernanda y Sus Amigos (CD)
> ❯ Clap along as this traditional song gets faster and faster.

What's for Supper? / ¿Qué hay para cenar? by Mary Risk, illustrated by Carol
Thompson, translated by Rosa Martín
> ● A family goes together to the grocery store to buy the ingredients for a
> supper surprise! Written in English and Spanish with very short sentences,
> the book can be read in both languages. A short picture dictionary is included.

Yum! ¡MmMm! ¡Qué rico! America's Sproutings by Pat Mora, illustrated by Rafael
López; translated by Pat Mora as *Yum! ¡MmMm! ¡Qué rico! Brotes de las
Américas*
> ● A collection of haikus introduces various foods native to the Americas.

Relevant Websites

Nourish Interactive
http://es.nourishinteractive.com/
> ● This website is dedicated to children's nutrition. Find recipes, games, print-
> ables, and more. Viewable in English as well.

YouTube: Boone County Public Library—Pin Pon
www.youtube.com/watch?v=ln4GxCtqikk
> ● Adriana demonstrates singing this traditional song with a puppet.

**AGE
RANGE**
Mixed Age /
Family

PROGRAM TITLE	DEVELOPED BY	THEME
**¡Cantamos cuentos! /
Let's Sing Stories!**	Katie Scherrer and Jamie
Campbell Naidoo	Music /
La música

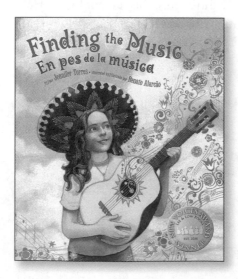

Opening Routine

"¿Cómo te llamas?" from *Basho and Friends en Español* by Basho and Friends
(CD)
> ❯ This Spanish song asks group members their names, how they feel, and where they live. After singing the song together, allow the children one by one to tell the group their name, how they feel, and where they live.

Book

Tito Puente, Mambo King / Tito Puente, Rey del mambo by Monica Brown, illustrated by Rafael López, translated by Adriana Domínguez
> ❯ One of the world's most beloved musicians is profiled in this playful, energetic biography.

Music Activity

Dance to some of Tito Puente's wonderful mambo music. A suggested title is "Ran Kan Kan," available on many different records. Add egg shakers or maracas so the children can make music of their own along with Tito.

Book

Finding the Music / En pos de la música by Jennifer Torres, illustrated by Renato Alarcão, translated by Alexis Romay
> ❯ A young girl learns how her grandfather's mariachi music affected various people in her neighborhood as she travels from neighbor to neighbor trying to fix his broken vihuela. Because this story is likely too long to read bilingually, read in either Spanish or English, mixing in some vocabulary words from the other language along the way.

Movement Song

"Mi cuerpo hace música" from *El doble de amigos / Twice as Many Friends* by Sol y Canto (CD)
> ❯ Find the various parts of the body as you use them to make music.

Book

Drum Dream Girl by Margarita Engle, illustrated by Rafael López
> ❯ This poem presents the inspiring story of Milo Castro Zaldarriaga, a multiracial girl in Cuba, who has an incredible talent for playing the drums at a time when it is taboo for girls to do so.

Closing Routine

"Adiós amigos" to the tune of "Diez deditos"

Adiós amigos
___

Adiós, adiós, adiós amigos.
Adiós, adiós, adiós amigos.
Adiós, adiós, adiós amigos.
¡Adiós amigos, adiós!

Extension Activity

Musical Instrument Play

INSTRUCTIONS

Have photos of different musical instruments. Introduce the names of the instruments in English and Spanish. Play sound clips of each instrument; samples of many instrument sounds are available from the San Francisco Symphony Kids' Site (www.sfskids.org/classic/templates/instorchframe.asp?pageid=3). Encourage adult caregivers to talk with their children about how the instruments are similar and different. Play sample sound clips of several instruments and have the group guess which instrument made the sound. If possible, provide a few real instruments (purchased or homemade) that the children can take turns playing.

MATERIALS NEEDED

- Pictures of various musical instruments
- Sound clips of various musical instruments
- Speakers and audio equipment or a tablet on which to play the musical sounds
- Purchased or homemade instruments to play

Bonus Storytime Resources

Creepy Crawly Calypso by Tony Langham, illustrated by Debbie Harter; translated by María A. Pérez as *¡Mira quién toca calipso!*
> Dance and count your way through the rain forest with this fun, rhyming book.

Drum, Chavi, Drum! / ¡Toca, Chavi, Toca! by Mayra L. Dole, illustrated by Tonel
> ❯ Chavi, a young Cuban American girl, proves that she has a special talent for drumming.

A Hen, a Chick and a String Guitar by Margaret Reed MacDonald, illustrated by Sophie Fatus; translated by María A. Pérez as *Algarabia en la granja*
> ❯ A cumulative tale from Chile that begins with a hen and ends with sixteen different animals and a guitar.

My Name Is Celia / Me llamo Celia by Monica Brown, illustrated by Rafael López, translated by Alicia Fontán
> ❯ ¡Azúcar! Meet Celia Cruz, the queen of salsa!

Digital Learning Extension

ABC Music digital app by Peapod Labs
https://itunes.apple.com/us/app/abc-music/id420949855?mt=8
> ❯ Using a combination of photos and animated multicultural characters, this interactive musical app invites children on an exploration to learn about instruments and music from around the world. Available in both English and Spanish, the app includes videos that demonstrate the instruments being played as well as the functionality to sound out letter sounds. Storytime facilitators could distribute digital tablets to families and encourage them to explore the various musical instruments with their children.

Relevant Websites

Tito Puente, Mambo King Curriculum Guide
www.monicabrown.net/files/TitoPuentecurriculumguide.pdf
> ❯ This guide presents a number of activities to share with children before and after reading the book and includes several activity sheets.

YouTube: Jbrary—"Mi cuerpo hace música"
www.youtube.com/watch?v=uISDW8OzU3w
> ❯ This is a wonderful demonstration of this Spanish children's song presented by two children's librarians.

PROGRAM TITLE	DEVELOPED BY	THEME
Bilingüitos	Kelly Von Zee	¡Vamos a ir de viaje! / We're going on a trip!

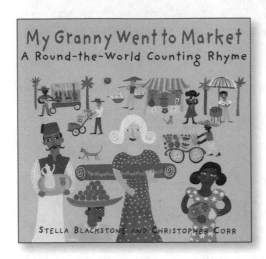

Opening Routine

"Buenos días amiguitos" from ¡Sabor! Spanish Learning Songs by Jorge Anaya (CD)

Bilingual Song

Sing to the tune of "If You're Happy and You Know It."

Si quieren leer un libro, aplaudir	If You Want to Read a Book, Clap Your Hands
Si quieren leer un libro, aplaudir. (clap, clap)	If you want to read a book, clap your hands. (clap, clap)
Si quieren leer un libro, aplaudir. (clap, clap)	If you want to read a book, clap your hands. (clap, clap)
Si quieren leer un libro, si quieren leer un libro,	If you want to read a book, if you want to read a book,
si quieren leer un libro, aplaudir. (clap, clap)	If you want to read a book, clap your hands. (clap, clap)

Book

El inesperado viaje de Mamut y Pingüino by Antonio Vicente, illustrated by Miguel Ordóñez
> ❯ A penguin and a mammoth who live at the North Pole need to move to the city and adjust to their new life.

Parachute Activity

Shake the parachute rápido/lento (fast/slow), arriba/abajo (up/down), lo más alto que puedan / lo más bajo que puedan (high as you can / low as you can). Spell the word *ciudad* (city) by throwing letter blocks one by one on the parachute and shaking them around. Go debajo (underneath) the parachute into a "casita," identify the colors on the parachute, count to ten, and . . . *afuera!*

Cleanup Song

"A limpiar / Let's Clean Up" from *¡Muévete! Learn Spanish through Song and Movement* by Spanish Playtime (CD)
> ❯ Encourage the children to help you put away the parachute and any other supplies used (such as blocks or balls) as you listen to the song.

Book

My Granny Went to Market: A Round-the-World Counting Rhyme by Stella Blackstone, illustrated by Christopher Corr; translated by Yanitzia Canetti as *Abuelita fue al mercado: Un libro en rima para contar por el mundo*
> ❯ Hop on the magic carpet and count your way around the world! Spanish translation maintains the rhyming text.

Traditional Song

Give the children ribbons or scarves of various colors to dance with while singing this song. Try drawing basic shapes or letters in the air with the ribbons or scarves.

De colores

De colores, de colores se visten los campos en la primavera.
De colores, de colores son los pajaritos que vienen de afuera.
De colores, de colores es el arco iris que vemos lucir.
Y por eso los grandes amores de muchos colores me gustan a mí (2x).

Goodbye Song

"Adiós, amigos" from *Diez Deditos: Ten Little Fingers and Other Play Rhymes and
Action Songs from Latin America* by José-Luis Orozco (CD)

Extension Activity

Map Making

INSTRUCTIONS

On a large piece of paper (such as a large section of butcher paper), write "El Polo
Norte / The North Pole" on one side and "La Ciudad / The City" on the other.
Invite the children and adults to draw on and color the "map." Encourage adults
to talk with the children about what happened in the story and how it feels to
go somewhere new.

MATERIALS NEEDED

- Large sheet of paper, such as butcher paper
- Art supplies for drawing and coloring, such as crayons, markers, and colored pencils

Bonus Storytime Resources

Lost and Found by Oliver Jeffers; translated by Jorge Luján as *Perdido y encontrado*
> A little boy travels far and wide to help a lost penguin who shows up at his
> door.

P is for Piñata: A Mexico Alphabet by Tony Johnston, illustrated by John Parra
> This rhyming, English-language alphabet story introduces the culture and
> traditions of Mexico.

"Vamos a la mar" from *De Colores and Other Latin-American Folk Songs for Children* by José-Luis Orozco (CD)
> Take a trip to the sea as you sing this fun Spanish song.

Digital Learning Extension

PBS Parents Play and Learn
http://pbskids.org/apps/pbs-parents-play--learn.html
> This free, bilingual (English/Spanish) app includes thirteen activities for
> building early math and literacy skills.

Relevant Website

StoryBlocks: De colores
www.storyblocks.org/videos/de-colores/
> ❯ This is a wonderful demonstration of this traditional Spanish song about colors.

PROGRAM TITLE	DEVELOPED BY	THEME
Bilingual Storytime / Cuentos bilingües	Melba Trujillo	Colors / Los colores

AGE RANGE
Mixed Age / Family

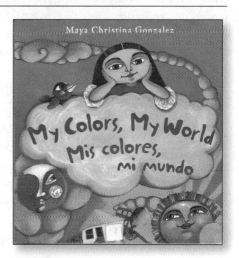

Opening Routine

Sing to the tune of "London Bridge" (from Preschool Rainbow at www.preschool rainbow.org/transition-rhymes.htm).

Hello Everybody	Hola a Todos
Hello everybody, yes, yes, yes,	Hola a todos, sí, sí, sí,
Yes, yes, yes,	sí, sí, sí,
Yes, yes, yes.	sí, sí, sí.
Hello everybody, yes, yes, yes,	Hola a todos, sí, sí, sí,
Yes, yes, yes, my friends.	sí, sí, sí mis amigos.

Book

Colores de la vida: Mexican Folk Art Colors in English and Spanish by
Cynthia Weill
> This bilingual book combines vibrant colors and wood carvings of animals
by artisans from the Mexican state of Oaxaca to teach children colors in English
and Spanish.

Traditional Song

Before singing this song, talk about colors and ask children what color the sun
is. If you know sign language, incorporate the signs for a few of the important
words as you sing, such as sun/sol, tree/árbol, children/niños, and play/jugar.
A Spanish version of this traditional song is available as "Señor Sol" from *En Mi
Casa* by Sing-A-Lingo.

Mister Sun

Oh Mister Sun, Sun, Mister golden Sun,
Please shine down on me.
Mister Sun, Sun, Mister golden Sun,
Hiding behind that tree.
These little children are asking you,
To please come out so we can play with you.
Oh Mister Sun, Sun, Mister golden Sun,
Please shine down on me.

Flannelboard Activity

Brown Bear, Brown Bear, What Do You See? by Bill Martin Jr., illustrated by Eric
Carle; translated by Teresa Mlawer as *Oso pardo, oso pardo, ¿qué ves ahí?*
> This story introduces animals of various colors while repeating the title
refrain. A printable flannelboard pattern based on this story can be found at
www.dltk-teach.com/books/brownbear/.

Traditional Rhyme

"Debajo de un botón / Martin Found a Mouse" from *¡Muu, Moo! Rimas de animales / Animal Nursery Rhymes* by Alma Flor Ada and F. Isabel Campoy,
illustrated by Viví Escrivá, English translation by Rosalma Zubizarreta
> Clap to the rhythm as you share this rhyme in Spanish and English.

Book

My Colors, My World / Mis colores, mi mundo by Maya Christina Gonzalez
> ❯ A little girl celebrates the magnificent colors that make up her world.

Flannelboard Activity

The Mouse behind the House / Ratoncita en la casita
> ❯ Create a flannelboard with a small mouse and a variety of houses of different colors. You can find several examples and a video demonstration at http://jbrary.com/little-mouse-little-mouse-renditions/. Hide the mouse behind a house and ask the children, "In what color house is the mouse hiding? De qué color es la casa en que se esconde el ratoncito?" Have a child come up, say the color in Spanish and English, and place a button by the house he picks. Then have all the children say, "Little Mouse, Little Mouse, are you in the (color) house? ¿Ratoncito, ratoncito, estás en la casa (color)?" Then have the child lift up the house and see if the mouse is hiding there. If the mouse is found before everyone has had a turn, hide the mouse again. Ask the child who found the mouse to hide the mouse for the next turn.

Closing Routine

"De colores" from *De Colores and Other Latin-American Folk Songs for Children* by José-Luis Orozco (CD)

Extension Activity

Color Bingo

INSTRUCTIONS

Make bingo cards with color dots or shapes and write the Spanish and English name for the color inside the color dot or shape. Laminate all the bingo cards. Make color strips, putting the Spanish and English name of the color on each strip. These are your color calling cards. Place the color calling cards in a small bag or box. As you pull out each strip, call out the color in Spanish and English. Children can mark their bingo cards with a crayon, dot paint marker, or small marker. This game was adapted from "Spanish Bingo to Learn Color Words in Spanish" (www.scribd.com/doc/13245405/spanish-bingo-to-learn-color-words-in-spanish#scribd).

- White card stock
- Small bag or box
- Crayons, small markers, or dot paint markers
- Templates

Bonus Storytime Resources

Colors! ¡Colores! by Jorge Luján, illustrated by Piet Grobler, translated by John Oliver Simon and Rebecca Parfitt
> ❯ Short, bilingual poems use imagery from the natural world to introduce the colors.

De colores / Bright with Colors by David Diaz
> ❯ This is a beautifully illustrated, bilingual picture book presentation of this traditional song.

Relevant Websites

¡Colorín Colorado! Meet the Author: José-Luis Orozco
www.colorincolorado.org/read/meet/orozco/
> ❯ Learn a little about children's musician José-Luis Orozco and find videos of him singing several of his most popular songs, including "De colores."

Sunflower Storytime: Mr. Sun in Sign Language
https://sunflowerstorytime.files.wordpress.com/2011/03/mr-sun-sign-language.pdf
> ❯ This PDF teaches the sign language for the "Mr. Sun" song.

YouTube: Washington County Cooperative Library System—"Debajo del botón"
www.youtube.com/watch?v=PyRpkq-ay5w
> ❯ Watch a video demonstration of this traditional rhyme.

PROGRAM TITLE	DEVELOPED BY	THEME
Bilingual Storytime / Cuentos bilingües	Melba Trujillo	Friendship / La amistad

Opening Routine

"Hola, Hola, Hola . . . It Means Hello" from *Bilingual Songs for Children* by Rosie and Andy (CD)

❯ Introduce the Spanish word *hola* with this bilingual educational sing-along. After singing the song, have the children say their names and shake hands with all their new friends.

Book

Gracias/Thanks by Pat Mora, illustrated by John Parra, translated by Adriana Domínguez

❯ This endearing book, written in both Spanish and English, is narrated by a young boy who is thankful for a best friend, his little brother, chocolate syrup, and so many wonderful, everyday things in our world.

Movement Song

"Si tú estás contento / If You're Happy and You Know It" from *Muévete: Learn Spanish through Song and Movement* by Spanish Playtime (CD)

❯ This fun Spanish song introduces body vocabulary and simple movements.

Storytelling Activity

El gallo de bodas / The Bossy Gallito

> This traditional folktale is wonderful to tell aloud. On his way through the forest to a wedding, a bossy little rooster learns that he can make more friends with kindness than with bossiness. Puppets or flannelboard pieces can be used to add a visual element to the storytelling. Tell bilingually with two presenters, go back and forth between English and Spanish with one presenter, or tell predominantly in one language, mixing in key vocabulary for the other.

Fingerplay Song

Count along on your fingers while singing this song to the tune of "Diez deditos."

Diez amigos	Ten Good Friends
Uno, dos, tres amigos.	One (and) two (and) three good friends.
Cuatro, cinco, seis amigos.	Four (and) five (and) six good friends.
Siete, ocho, nueve amigos.	Seven (and) eight (and) nine good friends.
¡Diez amigos somos!	Ten good friends are we!

Book

Little Beauty by Anthony Browne; translated by Teresa Mlawer as *Cosita linda*

> A powerful and unusual friendship is formed between a gorilla and a kitten.

Closing Routine

"Make New Friends" by Girl Scouts of America; Spanish translation from Mama Lisa's World (www.mamalisa.com/blog/the-song-make-new-friends-in-spanish-and-french/)

Make New Friends	Háganse nuevos amigos
Make new friends, but keep the old. One is silver and the other gold.	Háganse nuevos amigos, pero guarden los viejos. Uno es de plata y el otro es de oro.

Extension Activity

Friendship Wreath / Corona de la amistad

INSTRUCTIONS

Have adults help trace children's hands on construction paper. Children can then practice their own cutting skills or have adult help. Have the children write their names on their paper hands. Then put all the paper hands together to create a friendship wreath for the storytime area. Find detailed instructions in English at www.dltk-kids.com/crafts/friendship/mwreath.htm and in Spanish at www.dltk-ninos.com/manualidades/amigos/corona.htm.

MATERIALS NEEDED

- Construction paper
- Scissors
- Pencils
- Markers or crayons
- Glue

Bonus Storytime Resources

El gallo de bodas / The Bossy Gallito by Lucía M. González, illustrated by Lulu Delacre
> This fun, bilingual retelling of the traditional folktale is a great choice to read aloud or to use for storytelling.

Margaret and Margarita / Margarita y Margaret by Lynn Reiser
> Margaret speaks only English, and Margarita speaks only Spanish. Despite the language barrier, they become friends and have fun playing in the park.

Mis amigos / My Friends by Taro Gomi; originally published in Japanese as *Minna ga oshiete kuremashita*
> From her animal friends, a little girl learns to hop, run, walk, and do many other movements.

Relevant Websites

Miss Mary Liberry: Flannel Friday! *The Bossy Gallito / El gallo de bodas*
https://missmaryliberry.wordpress.com/2011/09/30/flannel-friday-the-bossy-gallitoel-gallo-de-bodas/
> This blog post includes a flannelboard pattern for this story.

YouTube: *El Gallo de bodas / The Bossy Gallito*
https://www.youtube.com/watch?v=n1wKmdtRMvE
>   Katie (Cunningham) Scherrer shares this example of bilingual flannelboard
storytelling.

Pat Mora: Ideas! and Curriculum Activities—*Gracias/Thanks*
www.patmora.com/ideas/#gracias
>   The well-known poet and author lists several fun activities to accompany
this book.

AGE RANGE
Mixed Age / Family

PROGRAM TITLE	DEVELOPED BY	THEME
Holiday Celebrations / Días festivos	Katie Scherrer and Jamie Campbell Naidoo	El Día de los Muertos / The Day of the Dead (November 1 and 2)

Opening Routine

"¡Hola, hola, hola!" from *Baile y canto* by Maria Fernanda y Sus Amigos (CD)
>   After singing the welcome song, talk together as a group about the Día
de los Muertos / Day of the Dead holiday. This is a festive and joyful time for
remembering our loved ones who have passed away.

Book

The Day of the Dead / El Día de los Muertos by Bob Barner, translated by Teresa
Mlawer
>   This bilingual introduction to this celebratory day rhymes in both English
and Spanish.

Movement Song

"Shake Them Bones" from *Dream a Little / Sueña un poquito* by Nathalia Palis (CD)

> • Shake your bones to this upbeat, bilingual tune with a rockabilly beat.

Book

Mi familia calaca / My Skeleton Family by Cynthia Weill, illustrated by Jesús Canseco Zárate

> • Meet the family in this fun spin on the traditional skeletons associated with the Day of the Dead.

Movement Song

"A bailar" from *¡Fantástico!* by Lucky Diaz and the Family Jam Band (CD)

> • This lively Spanish song will get everyone dancing and moving to the beat!

Book

Día de los Muertos by Roseanne Greenfield Thong, illustrated by Carles Ballesteros

> • Rhythmic text and vibrant illustrations introduce this holiday and its many traditions. Spanish words are blended in and contextually defined.

Closing Routine

"Adiós" from *Baile y canto* by Maria Fernanda y Sus Amigos (CD)

Extension Activity

Create a Día de los Muertos Altar

INSTRUCTIONS

A Día de los Muertos tradition is to create an altar that celebrates loved ones who have passed away. Altars are in a prominent area of the home for a few days before and after the holiday. Create a community altar using a large box, a table, or even a book cart. Cover with a tablecloth and decorate with traditional items such as marigolds, candles, papel picado (paper cut into elaborate designs), sugar skulls, and pan de muertos (a traditional holiday bread). Invite community members to share photos and favorite foods of loved ones on the community altar and display the altar in a prominent area of the library.

MATERIALS NEEDED

- A box, table, or book cart to use as the base of the altar
- Tablecloth
- Flowers (usually marigolds, but children can also make paper flowers for the altar)
- Sugar skulls (children can make these and add them to the altar)
- Photos of loved ones (invite community members to share photos and mementos of their loved ones on your altar; be sure to return all items after taking the altar down)

Bonus Storytime Resources

Calavera abecedario: A Day of the Dead Alphabet Book by Jeanette Winter
   ❯ The town gets ready for the Day of the Dead from A to Z.

The Dead Family Diaz by P. J. Bracegirdle, illustrated by Poly Bernatene
   ❯ Angelito is nervous for his first Day of the Dead when he will have to face the terrors that await in the Land of the Living!

Just a Minute: A Trickster Tale and Counting Book by Yuyi Morales
   ❯ Señor Calavera comes to take Grandma Beetle away, but she has a number of tricks up her sleeve. Craft patterns for masks and stick puppets are available on the author's website (www.srcalavera.com/chupirul.html).

Los Gatos Black on Halloween by Marisa Montes, illustrated by Yuyi Morales
   ❯ Combining elements of Halloween and the Day of the Dead, this sophisticated rhyming picture book introduces children to a host of famous Latin Americans. Face masks of the spooky characters can be downloaded for craft time from the illustrator's website (www.yuyimorales.com/gatosblack/gatos _black.html).

Digital Learning Extension

Rosita y Conchita in 3D—A Peek 'n' Play Story App by Mobad Games
https://itunes.apple.com/us/app/rosita-y-conchita-in-3d-peek/
   id535350585?mt=8
   ❯ Designed to be a three-dimensional, interactive storybook, this bilingual digital app introduces children to twin sisters who are separated by death and only reunited each year during Día de los Muertos. Through a series of actions, readers help the sisters come together to celebrate the holiday and their love for each other. Storytime leaders can display the app on the overhead screen and read the story. Alternatively, presenters can distribute digital tablets, and children can work in pairs or with their families to help the characters while listening to a narration of the story, which is available in Spanish or English.

Relevant Websites

Smithsonian Latino Center: Theater of the Dead
http://latino.si.edu/DayoftheDead/
> ❯ Enter the museum's interactive resource about the Día de los Muertos holiday.

YouTube: Sunny Earth Academy—"Chumba la cachumba"
https://www.youtube.com/watch?v=dVxOyjFRjAc
> ❯ Check out this upbeat song about calaveras.

NOTE

1. From *Baby Storytime Magic: Active Early Literacy through Bounces, Rhymes, Tickles, and More* by Kathy MacMillan and Christine Kirker (Chicago: ALA Editions, 2014).

Chapter Seven

Recommended Professional Resources and Children's Media for Bilingual Programming

his chapter provides extensive lists of recommended print and digital professional resources and children's materials for librarians and others interested in planning engaging bilingual storytimes and selecting Latino children's literature. We include a bibliography of all children's books used in the sample program plans as well as other children's books and music CDs ideal for bilingual programming.

PROFESSIONAL PRINT RESOURCES

Ada, Alma Flor. *Alma Flor Ada and You: Volume One*. Westport, CT: Libraries Unlimited, 2005.

———. *Alma Flor Ada and You: Volume Two*. Westport, CT: Libraries Unlimited, 2008.

Alire, Camilla A., and Jacqueline Ayala. *Serving Latino Communities: A How-to-Do-It Manual for Librarians*. 2nd ed. New York: Neal-Schuman, 2007.

Avila, Salvador. *Crash Course in Serving Spanish-Speakers*. Westport, CT: Libraries Unlimited, 2008.

Ayala, John, and Salvador Güereña. *Pathways to Progress: Issues and Advances in Latino Librarianship*. Westport, CT: Libraries Unlimited, 2010.

Baumann, Susana. *¡Hola, amigos! A Plan for Latino Outreach*. Santa Barbara, CA: Libraries Unlimited, 2010.

Byrd, Susannah Mississippi. *¡Bienvenidos! ¡Welcome! A Handy Resource Guide for Marketing Your Library to Latinos*. Chicago: American Library Association, 2005.

Campos, David. *Learning from Latino Role Models: Inspire Students through Biographies, Instructional Activities, and Creative Assignments.* Lanham, MD: Rowman and Littlefield, 2016.

Clark, Ellen Riojas, Belinda Bustos Flores, Howard L. Smith, and Daniel Alejandro González, eds. *Multicultural Literature for Latino Bilingual Children: Their Words, Their Worlds.* Lanham, MD: Rowman and Littlefield, 2015.

Diamant-Cohen, Betsy. *Early Literacy Programming en Español: Mother Goose on the Loose Programs for Bilingual Learners.* New York: Neal-Schuman, 2010.

Immroth, Barbara, and Kathleen de la Peña McCook. *Library Services to Youth of Hispanic Heritage.* Jefferson, NC: McFarland, 2000.

King, K. A., and A. Mackey. *The Bilingual Edge: Why, When, and How to Teach Your Child a Second Language.* New York: HarperCollins, 2007.

Moller, Sharon Chickering. *Library Services to Spanish Speaking Patrons: A Practical Guide.* Englewood, CO: Libraries Unlimited, 2001.

Naidoo, Jamie Campbell, ed. *Celebrating Cuentos: Promoting Latino Children's Literature and Literacy in Classrooms and Libraries.* Santa Barbara, CA: Libraries Unlimited, 2011.

Pavon, Ana-Elba, and Diana Borrego. *25 Latino Craft Projects.* Chicago: American Library Association, 2002.

Treviño, Rose Zertuche. *The Pura Belpré Awards: Celebrating Latino Authors and Illustrators.* Chicago: American Library Association, 2006.

———. *Read Me a Rhyme in Spanish and English / Léame una rima en español e inglés.* Chicago: American Library Association, 2009.

Vardell, Sylvia, and Janet Wong. *The Poetry Friday Anthology for Celebrations: Holiday Poems for the Whole Year in English and Spanish.* Teacher/Librarian Edition. Princeton, NJ: Pomelo Books, 2015.

Wadham, Tim. *Programming with Latino Children's Materials: A How-to-Do-It Manual for Librarians.* New York: Neal-Schuman, 1999.

ONLINE RESOURCES

Many libraries and other organizations are working to creatively share the joy of reading and the importance of early literacy with Spanish-speaking families. The following resources can provide inspiration as you develop your own bilingual storytime program and communicate early literacy messages to parents.

Library Resources

Anaheim (California) Libraries YouTube Channel
www.youtube.com/user/AnaheimLibraries
Look for the "Storytime videos" playlist for more than twenty bilingual stories and songs.

Arlington County (Virginia) Library YouTube Channel: Cuentos y más
www.youtube.com/user/arlingtoncounty
This bilingual storytime television show is from the Arlington County (Virginia) Library. Find all episodes on the "Cuentos y más" playlist.

Brooklyn (New York) Public Library: Ready, Set, Kindergarten! Español
www.bklynlibrary.org/first-5-years/ready-set-kindergarten-español-spanish
This website has early literacy information, tips, and videos for parents in Spanish.

Colorado Libraries for Early Literacy: StoryBlocks
www.storyblocks.org
In the Languages menu, select "Español" for multiple video demonstrations of traditional Spanish-language rhymes and songs.

Johnson County (Kansas) Library YouTube Channel
www.youtube.com/user/jocolibrary
Look for the "Juego de manitos (6 by 6 Finger Plays En Español)" playlist for video demonstrations of Spanish-language fingerplays.

**King County (Washington) Library System: Tell Me a Story—
    World Languages**
http://tmas.kcls.org/category/World_Languages/
This site has lyrics and video demonstrations of songs and rhymes in many languages, including an extensive Spanish collection.

**Washington County (Oregon) Cooperative Library Services: Rimas en
    español**
www.wccls.org/es/rimas
Early literacy information for parents and many Spanish rhyme demonstrations can be found here.

Worthington (Ohio) Libraries
www.worthingtonlibraries.org/interact/av/topics/espanol
This site has audio versions of Spanish and bilingual songs, rhymes, and stories.

Early Literacy Resources

**Center for Early Literacy Learning: Spanish Practice Guides for Use with
    Parents**
http://earlyliteracylearning.org/pgparents_span.php
Find guides and activities to help Spanish-speaking parents promote early literacy.

Children's Museum of Houston: Para los niños

www.cmhouston.org/para-los-ninos

This site offers English and Spanish resources from this family literacy program designed for Spanish-speaking families.

Chile Crece Contigo

www.crececontigo.gob.cl

This well-designed government website from Chile helps parents support their child's physical, emotional, and mental development during the first years of life.

¡Colorín Colorado!

www.colorincolorado.org

This bilingual website has materials and resources for the families and educators of English language learners.

Cuentos y Más / Stories and More

http://tv.arlingtonva.us/videos/cuentos-y-mas

This bilingual literacy program, produced in part by the Arlington County (Virginia) Public Library, promotes reading among both English- and Spanish-speaking children.

DayByDayVA: Calendario de alfabetización familiar

http://sp.daybydayva.org

On this online family literacy calendar, each day features a song, a video, a recommended book, and online resources.

Earlier Is Easier

www.espanol-eie.org

This collaborative project promotes early literacy among Denver families.

PBS Kids Lab

http://pbskids.org/lab/es

Videos, games, and activities to support early learning are presented in Spanish on this site.

Zero to Three: Early Experiences Matter

www.zerotothree.org/about-us/areas-of-expertise/free-parent-brochures
    -and-guides

This site provides parent handouts in English and Spanish.

Resources for Planning Bilingual Storytimes

Bilingual Storytime
http://bilingualstorytime.org
Contributor Kelly Von Zee maintains this blog of bilingual storytime ideas and plans.

El dia de los Niños / El dia de los libros (Children's Day / Book Day) or Día
http://dia.ala.org
Recommended booklists, activities, and marketing materials are available on this site for libraries interested in promoting Día in the library.

¡Es divertido hablar dos idiomas!
http://bilingualchildrensprogramming.blogspot.com
This blog by coauthor Katie Scherrer is dedicated to bilingual storytime resource sharing.

Pinterest: Flannel Friday—Bilingual
www.pinterest.com/flannelfriday/bilingual
This is a collection of bilingual flannelboards made by the participants of the Flannel Friday online group.

REFORMA: The National Association to Promote Library and Information Services to Latinos and the Spanish-Speaking—Children and Young Adult Resources
www.reforma.org/content.asp?contentid=87
Find information here on several topics related to serving Latino children and youth in libraries, including bilingual storytime.

Texas State Library and Archives Commission: Dígame un cuento / Tell Me a Story
www.tsl.texas.gov/ld/pubs/bilingual/index.html
This site has multiple sample bilingual storytime plans.

Utah State Library: Bilingual Storytimes
http://heritage.utah.gov/library/spanish-bilingual-storytimes
Tips, books, and scripts for planning bilingual storytimes are available on this site.

Educational and Entertaining Spanish-Language Resources for Families

Mundo VeoVeo

http://mundoveoveo.gob.ec/web

This is the website for a children's television channel maintained by Ecuador's Ministry of Economic and Social Inclusion.

Paka Paka

www.pakapaka.gob.ar

This is the website for a children's television channel maintained by Argentina's Ministry of Education.

Plaza Sésamo

www.plazasesamo.com

The Spanish-language *Sesame Street* website has videos and activities for kids as well as helpful information for parents.

Other Resources

La Bloga

http://labloga.blogspot.com

Created by Rudy García, Manuel Ramos, and Michael Sedano, this blog is dedicated to providing reviews, news, and interviews related to Latino publishing (including Latino children's literature).

Los Bloguitos

www.losbloguitos.com

This Spanish-language blog, created by Latino authors and illustrators, includes stories, songs, poems, and more for children.

De Colores: The Raza Experience in Books for Children

http://decoloresreviews.blogspot.com

Developed by Beverly Slapin and several other reviewers of Latino children's books, this blog critically examines Latino children's materials.

Comienza en Casa / "It Starts at Home"

www.manomaine.org/programs/mep/comienzaencasa

This bilingual education program, sponsored by the Maine Migrant Education Program and Mano en Mano / Hand in Hand, uses iPads and digital apps to help Spanish-speaking preschoolers learn English.

Latin Baby Book Club
www.latinbabybookclub.com
This useful blog is dedicated to highlighting Latino children's literature and providing interviews with notable Latino authors and illustrators.

Latinas for Latino Lit
http://latinas4latinolit.org
This site promotes Latino children's literature and literacy through its flagship program, the L4LL Latino Children's Summer Reading Program.

Latinos in Kid Lit
http://latinosinkidlit.com
This site provides frequently updated information about Latino children's literature, including a database of books by Latino authors and illustrators.

Spanish in Our Libraries and Public Libraries Using Spanish
www.sol-plus.net
This site has numerous resources for libraries serving Spanish-speaking populations, including library signage in Spanish.

MATERIALS USED IN SAMPLE STORYTIMES

All the CDs and books referenced in the sample storytime plans in chapter 6 are listed in this section. Also listed are recommended titles by and about Latinos for English storytime, as well as recommended bilingual and Spanish titles not included in the program plans.

Music CDs

Anaya, Jorge. *¡A Bailar! / Let's Dance!*. Whistlefritz, 2008, compact disc.
———. *Cha, Cha, Cha Spanish Learning Songs*. Whistlefritz, 2010, compact disc.
———. *¡Sabor! Spanish Learning Songs*. Whistlefritz, 2014, compact disc.
Barchas, Sarah. *Piñata and More: Bilingual Songs for Children*. High Haven Music, 1997, compact disc.
Basho and Friends. *Basho and Friends en Español*. Self-released, 2012, compact disc.
Canticuénticos. *Canticuénticos Embrujados*. GOBI Music, 2009, compact disc.
Diaz, Lucky, and the Family Jam Band. *¡Fantástico!* BenMar Music/Rainy Day Dimes, 2013, compact disc.
Dorn, Susy. *Sal y Pimienta*. Self-released, 2008, compact disc.
Feldman, Jean. *Ole! Ole! Ole! Dr. Jean en Español*. Self-released, 2008, compact disc.

Fernanda, Maria, y Sus Amigos. *Baile y Canto*. Self-released, 2006, compact disc.

Juguemos a Cantar. *Baby's First Songs in Spanish*. St. Clair Entertainment, 2002, compact disc.

Manners, Beth. *Playtime Spanish for Kids*. Future Boomers Corp, 2006, compact disc.

Mister G. *ABC Fiesta*. Coil Records, 2013, compact disc.

Orozco, José-Luis. *De Colores and Other Latin-American Folk Songs for Children*. Arcoiris Records, 2009, compact disc.

———. *Diez Deditos: Ten Little Fingers and Other Play Rhymes and Action Songs from Latin America*. Arcoiris Records, 2004, compact disc.

Palis, Nathalia. *From Here to There*. Self-released, 2012, compact disc.

———. *Dream a Little / Sueña un poquito*. Self-released, 2014, compact disc.

Rahel, Evelio Mendez, and Betsy Diamant-Cohen. *Escucha y disfruta con Mama Gansa / Listen, Like, Learn with Mother Goose on the Loose en Español*. Betsy's Folly Studios, 2009, compact disc.

Rosie and Andy. *Bilingual Songs for Children*. Rosie and Andy, 2011, compact disc.

Sol y Canto. *El doble de amigos / Twice as Many Friends*. Rounder, 2009, compact disc.

Sing-A-Lingo. *En Mi Casa*. CD Baby, 2008, compact disc.

Spanish Playtime. *¡Muévete! Learn Spanish through Song and Movement*. Self-released, 2005, compact disc.

Spanish Together. *Play in Spanish*. Self-released, 2008, compact disc.

———. *Spanish All Year Round*. Self-released, 2012, compact disc.

Picture Books

Ada, Alma Flor. *Gathering the Sun: An Alphabet in Spanish and English*. Illustrated by Simon Silva. Translated by Rosalma Zubizarreta. New York: HarperCollins, 1997.

———. *Mamá Goose: Un Tesoro de rimas infantiles / A Latino Nursery Treasury*. Illustrated by Maribel Suárez. New York: Hyperion Books for Children, 2004.

Ada, Alma Flor, and F. Isabel Campoy. *Ten Little Puppies / Diez perritos*. Illustrated by Ulises Wensell. Translated by Rosalma Zubizarreta. New York: Rayo, 2011.

Amado, Elisa. *Why Are You Doing That?* Illustrated by Manuel Monroy. Toronto: Groundwood Books / House of Anansi Press, 2014.

Argueta, Jorge. *Arroz Con Leche: Un poema para cocinar / Rice Pudding: A Cooking Poem*. Illustrated by Fernando Vilela. Toronto: Groundwood Books, 2010.

———. *Salsa: Un poema para cocinar / Salsa: A Cooking Poem*. Illustrated by Duncan Tonatiuh. Translated by Elisa Amado. Toronto: Groundwood Books / House of Anansi Press, 2015.

Barner, Bob. *The Day of the Dead / El Día de los Muertos*. Translated by Teresa Mlawer. New York: Holiday House, 2010.

Beaton, Clare. *Cerdota grandota?* Illustrated by Stella Blackstone. Translated by Yanitzia Canetti. Cambridge, MA: Barefoot Books, 2007.

Bertrand, Diane Gonzales. *Somos primos / We Are Cousins.* Illustrated by Christina E. Rodriguez. Houston, TX: Piñata Books, 2007.

Blackstone, Stella. *Abuelita fue al mercado: Un libro en rima para contar por el mundo.* Illustrated by Christopher Corr. Translated by Yanitzia Canetti. Cambridge, MA: Barefoot Books, 2007.

Bracegirdle, P. J. *The Dead Family Diaz.* Illustrated by Poly Bernatene. New York: Dial Books for Young Readers, 2012.

Brown, Monica. *Marisol McDonald and the Clash Bash / Marisol McDonald y la fiesta sin igual.* Illustrated by Sara Palacios. Translated by Adriana Domínguez. New York: Children's Book Press, 2013.

———. *My Name Is Celia / Me llamo Celia.* Illustrated by Rafael López. Translated by Alicia Fontán. Flagstaff, AZ: Rising Moon, 2004.

———. *Tito Puente, Mambo King / Tito Puente, Rey del mambo.* Illustrated by Rafael López. Translated by Adriana Domínguez. New York: HarperCollins, 2013.

Browne, Anthony. *Cosita linda.* Translated by Teresa Mlawer. Somerville, MA: Candlewick, 2008.

Canetti, Yanitzia. *Uno, Dos, Tres: My First Spanish Rhymes.* Illustrated by Patrice Aggs. London: Frances Lincoln Children's Books, 2012.

Cisneros, Sandra. *Hairs / Pelitos.* Illustrated by Terry Ybáñez. Translated by Liliana Valenzuela. New York: Knopf, 1994.

Cumpiano, Ina. *Quinito's Neighborhood / El vecindario de Quinito.* Illustrated by José Ramírez. San Francisco: Children's Book Press, 2005.

Delacre, Lulu. *Arroz Con Leche: Popular Songs and Rhymes from Latin America.* New York: Scholastic, 1989.

Diaz, David. *De colores / Bright with Colors.* New York: Marshall Cavendish, 2008.

Dole, Mayra Lazara. *Drum, Chavi, Drum! / ¡Toca, Chavi, Toca!* Illustrated by Tonel. New York: Lee and Low Books, 2013.

Dominguez, Angela. *María tenía una llamita / Maria Had a Little Llama.* New York: Henry Holt, 2013.

Dorros, Arthur. *Abuela.* Illustrated by Raúl Colón. New York: Dutton Children's Books, 1991.

———. *Papá and Me.* Illustrated by Rudy Gutierrez. New York: Rayo, 2008.

Elya, Susan Middleton. *Little Roja Riding Hood.* Illustrated by Susan Guevara. New York: G. P. Putnam's Sons, 2014.

Emberley, Rebecca. *My Garden / Mi jardín.* New York: Little, Brown, 2005.

Engle, Margarita. *Drum Dream Girl.* Illustrated by Rafael López. Boston, New York: Houghton Mifflin Harcourt, 2015.

Fox, Mem. *Diez deditos de las manos y diez deditos de los pies / Ten Little Fingers and Ten Little Toes.* Illustrated by Helen Oxenbury. Translated by F. Isabel Campoy. Boston: Houghton Mifflin Harcourt, 2012.

Gomi, Taro. *Mis amigos / My Friends.* San Francisco: Chronicle Books, 2006.

González, Lucía M. *El gallo de bodas / The Bossy Gallito.* Illustrated by Lulu Delacre. New York: Scholastic, 1994.

Gonzalez, Maya Christina. *Call Me Tree / Llámame árbol.* New York: Children's Book Press, 2014.

———. *I Know the River Loves Me / Yo sé que el río me ama.* San Francisco: Children's Book Press, 2009.

_____. *My Colors, My World / Mis colores, mi mundo*. San Francisco: Children's Book Press, 2011.

Guy, Ginger Foglesong. *¡Fiesta!* Illustrated by René King Moreno. New York: Greenwillow Books, 1996.

_____. *¡Perros! ¡Perros! Dogs! Dogs!* Illustrated by Sharon Glick. New York: Greenwillow Books, 2006.

Harris, Jay. *The Moon Is La Luna: Silly Rhymes in English and Spanish*. Illustrated by Matthew Cordell. Boston: Houghton Mifflin, 2007.

Jeffers, Oliver. *Perdido y encontrado*. Translated by Jorge Luján. Mexico: Fondo de Cultura Económica, 2005.

Johnston, Tony. *P Is for Piñata: A Mexico Alphabet*. Illustrated by John Parra. Chelsea, MI: Sleeping Bear Press, 2008.

Kalan, Robert. *¡Salta, ranita, salta!* Illustrated by Byron Barton. Translated by Aída E. Marcuse. New York: HarperCollins, 1994.

Katz, Karen. *Where Is Baby's Bellybutton? / ¿Dónde está el ombliguito?* Translated by Argentina Palacios Ziegler. New York: Little Simon, 2002.

Knox, Barbara. *Bajo las olas 1, 2, 3 / Under the Sea 1, 2, 3*. Translated by Martin Luis Guzman Ferrer. Mankato, MN: Capstone Press Interactive, 2008.

Laínez, René Colato. *Señor Pancho Had a Rancho*. Illustrated by Elwood Smith. New York: Holiday House, 2013.

Langham, Tony. *Creepy Crawly Calypso*. Illustrated by Debbie Harter. Cambridge, MA: Barefoot Books, 2004.

Luján, Jorge. *Colors! ¡Colores!* Illustrated by Piet Grobler. Translated by John Oliver Simon and Rebecca Parfitt. Toronto: Groundwood Books/Libros Tigrillo, House of Anansi Press, 2008.

_____. *Rooster/Gallo*. Illustrated by Manuel Monroy. Translated by Elisa Amado. Toronto: Groundwood Books, 2004.

MacDonald, Margaret Reed. *Algarabia en la granja*. Illustrated by Sophie Fatus. Translated by María A. Pérez. Cambridge, MA: Barefoot Books, 2009.

Martin, Bill, Jr. *Brown Bear, Brown Bear, What Do You See? / Oso pardo, oso pardo, ¿qué ves ahí?* Illustrated by Eric Carle. Translated by Teresa Mlawer. New York: Henry Holt, 1998.

Martin, Bill, Jr., and Michael Sampson. *Amo nuestra tierra / I Love Our Earth*. Photographs by Dan Lipow. Translated by Yanitzia Canetti. Watertown, MA: Charlesbridge, 2013.

Masurel, Claire. *Un gato y un perro / A Cat and a Dog*. Illustrated by Bob Kolar. Translated by Andrés Antreasyan. New York: Ediciones Norte-Sur, 2003.

_____. *¡No, Tito, no! / No, No Titus!* Illustrated by Shari Halpern. Translated by Diego Lasconi. New York: North-South Books, 1999.

Montes, Marisa. *Los Gatos Black on Halloween*. Illustrated by Yuyi Morales. New York: Henry Holt, 2006.

Mora, Pat. *Book Fiesta! Celebrate Children's Day, Book Day / Celebremos El día de los niños, El día de los libros*. Illustrated by Rafael López. New York: HarperCollins, 2009.

_____. *Gracias / Thanks*. Illustrated by John Parra. Translated by Adriana Domínguez. New York: Lee and Low Books, 2009.

————. *Let's Eat! / ¡A comer!* Illustrated by Maribel Suárez. New York: HarperCollins, 2008.

————. *Sweet Dreams / Dulces sueños.* Illustrated by Maribel Suárez. New York: Rayo, 2008.

————. *Water Rolls, Water Rises / El agua rueda, el agua sube.* Illustrated by Meilo So. Translated by Adriana Domínguez. New York: Children's Book Press, 2014.

————. *Wiggling Pockets / Los bolsillos saltarines.* Illustrated by Maribel Suárez. New York: Rayo, 2009.

————. *Yum! ¡MmMm! ¡Qué rico! America's Sproutings.* Illustrated by Rafael López. New York: Lee and Low Books, 2007.

Morales, Yuyi. *Just a Minute: A Trickster Tale and Counting Book.* San Francisco: Chronicle Books, 2003.

Pinto and Chinto. *Nicomedes el pelón.* Sevilla: Kalandraka, 2013.

Reiser, Lynn. *Margaret and Margarita / Margarita y Margaret.* New York: Greenwillow Books, 1993.

Risk, Mary. *What's for Supper? / ¿Qué hay para cenar?* Illustrated by Carol Thompson. Translated by Rosa Martín. Hauppauge, NY: Barron's, 1998.

Rosales-Yeomans, Natalia. *Canta, Rana, canta / Sing, Froggie, Sing.* Illustrated by Carolyn Dee Flores. Houston, TX: Piñata Books, 2013.

Ruesga, Rita Rosa. *Cantaba la rana / The Frog Was Singing.* Illustrated by Soledad Sebastián. New York: Scholastic, 2011.

————. *La piñata / The Piñata.* Illustrated by Soledad Sebastián. New York: Scholastic, 2012.

Ryan, Pam Muñoz. *Hello Ocean / Hola mar.* Illustrated by Mark Astrella. Translated by Yanitzia Canetti. Watertown, MA: Charlesbridge, 2003.

Saldaña, René, Jr. *Dale, dale, dale: Una fiesta de números / Hit It, Hit It, Hit It: A Fiesta of Numbers.* Illustrated by Carolyn Dee Flores. Houston, TX: Piñata Books, 2013.

Smith, Lane. *El jardín del abuelo.* Translated by Paulina de Aguinaco Martin. Mexico: Océano de México, 2012.

Tafolla, Carmen. *Fiesta Babies.* Illustrated by Amy Córdova. Berkeley, CA: Tricycle Press, 2010.

Thong, Roseanne Greenfield. *Día de los Muertos.* Illustrated by Carles Ballesteros. Chicago: Albert Whitman, 2015.

————. *Green Is a Chile Pepper.* Illustrated by John Parra. San Francisco: Chronicle Books, 2014.

Tonatiuh, Duncan. *Dear Primo: A Letter to My Cousin.* New York: Abrams Books for Young Readers, 2010.

Torres, Jennifer. *Finding the Music / En pos de la música.* Illustrated by Renato Alarcão. Translated by Alexis Romay. New York: Children's Book Press, 2015.

Vamos, Samantha. *The Cazuela That the Farm Maiden Stirred.* Illustrated by Rafael López. Watertown, MA: Charlesbridge, 2011.

Vicente, Antonio. *El inesperado viaje de Mamut y Pingüino.* Illustrated by Miguel Ordóñez. Zaragoza, Spain: Edelvives, 2013.

Walsh, Ellen Stoll. *Salta y brinca.* Translated by Alma Flor Ada and F. Isabel Campoy. San Diego: Libros Viajeros, Harcourt Brace, 1996.

Weill, Cynthia. *Colores de la vida: Mexican Folk Art Colors in English and Spanish.* El Paso, TX: Cinco Puntos Press, 2011.

_____. *Mi familia calaca / My Skeleton Family.* Illustrated Jesús Canseco Zárate. El Paso, TX: Cinco Puntos Press, 2013.

_____. *Opuestos: Mexican Folk Art Opposites in English and Spanish.* Artwork by Quirino and Martín Santiago. El Paso, TX: Cinco Puntos Press, 2009.

Winter, Jeanette. *Calavera abecedario: A Day of the Dead Alphabet Book.* Orlando, FL: Harcourt, 2004.

CHILDREN'S BOOKS BY AND ABOUT LATINOS FOR ENGLISH-LANGUAGE STORYTIMES

Ada, Alma Flor. *I Love Saturdays y Domingos.* Illustrated by Elivia Savadier. New York: Atheneum Books for Young Readers, 2002.

Amado, Elisa. *What Are You Doing?* Illustrated by Manuel Monroy. Toronto: Groundwood Books/House of Anansi Press, 2011.

_____. *Why Are You Doing That?* Illustrated by Manuel Monroy. Toronto: Groundwood Books/House of Anansi Press, 2014.

Arena, Jen. *Besos for Baby: A Little Book of Kisses.* Illustrated by Blanca Gómez. New York: LB Kids, 2014.

Brown, Monica. *Waiting for the Biblioburro.* Illustrated by John Parra. Berkeley, CA: Tricycle Press, 2011.

Deedy, Carmen Agra. *Martina the Beautiful Cockroach: A Cuban Folktale.* Illustrated by Michael Austin. Atlanta, GA: Peachtree, 2007.

Dorros, Arthur. *Abuelo.* Illustrated by Raúl Colón. New York: Harper, 2014.

_____. *Mamá and Me.* Illustrated by Rudy Gutierrez. New York: Rayo, 2011.

Garza, Xavier. *The Great and Mighty Nikko.* El Paso, TX : Cinco Puntos Press, 2015.

Johnston, Tony. *My Abuelita.* Illustrated by Yuyi Morales. Boston: Houghton Mifflin Harcourt, 2009.

Laínez, René Colato. *The Tooth Fairy Meets El Ratón Pérez.* Illustrated by Tom Lintern. Berkeley, CA: Tricycle Press, 2010.

Luján, Jorge. *Moví la mano / I Moved My Hand.* Illustrated by Mandana Sadat. Translated by Elisa Amado. Toronto: Groundwood Books/House of Anansi Press, 2014.

MacDonald, Margaret Read. *Conejito: A Folktale from Panama.* Illustrated by Geraldo Valério. Little Rock, AR : August House LittleFolk, 2006.

Medina, Meg. *Mango, Abuela, and Me.* Illustrated by Angela Dominguez. Somerville, MA: Candlewick, 2015.

_____. *Tía Isa Wants a Car.* Illustrated by Claudio Muñoz. Somerville, MA: Candlewick, 2011.

Montes, Marisa. *Juan Bobo Goes to Work: A Puerto Rican Folk Tale.* Illustrated by Joe Cepeda. New York: HarperCollins, 2000.

Mora, Pat. *Doña Flor: A Tall Tale about a Giant Woman with a Great Big Heart.* Illustrated by Raúl Colón. New York: Knopf, 2005.

————. *¡Marimba! Animales from A to Z.* Illustrated by Doug Cushman. New York: Clarion Books, 2006.

————. *A Piñata in a Pine Tree: A Latino Twelve Days of Christmas.* Illustrated by Magaly Morales. Boston: Clarion Books, 2009.

————. *The Race of Toad and Deer.* Illustrated by Domi. Toronto: Douglas and McIntyre, 2001.

Morales, Yuyi. *Just in Case: A Trickster Tale and Spanish Alphabet Book.* New York: Roaring Brook Press, 2008.

————. *Niño Wrestles the World.* New York: A Neal Porter Book, 2013.

Tafolla, Carmen. *What Can You Do with a Paleta?* Illustrated by Magaly Morales. Berkeley, CA: Tricycle Press, 2009.

————. *What Can You Do with a Rebozo?* Illustrated by Amy Córdova. Berkeley, CA: Tricycle Press, 2008.

Thong, Roseanne Greenfield. *Round Is a Tortilla: A Book of Shapes.* Illustrated by John Parra. San Francisco: Chronicle Books, 2013.

————. *'Twas Nochebuena: A Christmas Story in English and Spanish.* Illustrated by Sara Palacios. New York: Viking, 2014.

Tonatiuh, Duncan. *Funny Bones: Posada and His Day of the Dead Calaveras.* New York: Abrams Books for Young Readers, 2015.

Weeks, Sarah. *Counting Ovejas.* Illustrated by David Diaz. New York: Atheneum Books for Young Readers, 2006.

BILINGUAL AND SPANISH-LANGUAGE CHILDREN'S BOOKS FOR BILINGUAL STORYTIMES

Brown, Monica. *Maya's Blanket: La manta de Maya.* Illustrated by David Diaz. New York: Children's Book Press, 2015.

Campoy, F. Isabel. *Mi día de la A a la Z.* Miami, FL: Alfaguara/Santillana USA, 2009.

Costales, Amy. *Hello Night / Hola Noche.* Flagstaff, AZ: Luna Rising, 2007.

Cumpiano, Ina. *Quinito, Día y Noche / Quinito, Day and Night.* San Francisco: Children's Book Press, 2008.

Delacre, Lulu. *Arroró, mi Niño: Latino Lullabies and Gentle Games.* New York: Lee and Low Books, 2004.

Garza, Carmen Lomas. *Family Picture / Cuadros de Familia.* 15th anniversary ed. San Francisco: Children's Book Press, 2005.

Gomi, Taro. *Llegó la Primavera / Spring Is Here.* San Francisco: Chronicle Books, 2006.

González, Lucía. *The Storyteller's Candle / La Velita de los Cuentos.* Illustrated by Lulu Delacre. San Francisco: Children's Book Press, 2008.

Gribel, Christiane. *No Voy a Dormir / I Am Not Going to Sleep.* Illustrated by Orlando. New York: Lectorum Publications, 2009.

Guy, Ginger Foglesong. *Bravo!* Illustrated by Rene King Moreno. New York: Greenwillow Books, 2010.

_____. *Siesta*. Illustrated by Rene King Moreno. New York: Greenwillow Books, 2005.

Hall, Nancy A., and Jill Syverson-Stork. *Los pollitos dicen / The Baby Chicks Sing: Juegos, rimas y canciones infantiles de países de habla hispana / Traditional Games, Nursery Rhymes, and Songs from Spanish-Speaking Countries*. Illustrated by Kay Chorao. Boston: Little, Brown, 1994.

Lacámara, Laura. *Dalia's Wondrous Hair / El maravilloso cabello de Dalia*. Houston, TX: Arte Público Press/Piñata Books, 2014.

Laínez, René Colato. *Playing Loteria / El Juego de la Loteria*. Flagstaff, AZ: Luna Rising, 2005.

Mora, Pat. *Uno, Dos, Tres / One, Two, Three*. Illustrated by Barbara Lavallee. New York: Clarion Books, 1996.

Morales, Yuyi. *Viva Frida*. Photographs by Tim O'Meara. New York: Roaring Brook Press, 2014.

Orozco, José-Luis. *De colores and Other Latin American Folk Songs for Children*. Illustrated by Elisa Kleven. New York: Penguin Putnam, 1999.

_____. *Diez deditos and Other Play Rhymes and Action Songs from Latin America*. Illustrated by Elisa Kleven. New York: Puffin, 2002.

_____. *Fiestas: A Year of Latin American Songs of Celebration*. Illustrated by Elisa Kleven. New York: Dutton/Penguin Putnam, 2002.

Weill, Cynthia. *Count Me In*. Illustrated by Guillermina Aguilar, Josefina Aguilar, Irene Aguilar, and Concepción Aguilar. El Paso, TX: Cinco Puntos Press, 2012.

Wellington, Monica. *Apple Farmer Annie / Ana Cultiva Manzanas*. New York: Dutton Children's Books, 2004.

Zapata, Andres. *Los Pollitos*. Broomall, PA: Mason Reads, 2012.

About the Contributors

Adriana Silva was born and raised in Mexico and got her BA in pedagogy in 1998. She came to Kentucky in 2006 with her husband and daughter. To fulfill her interest in serving the growing Hispanic community in her county, Adriana has been providing library and information services through outreach and family programs at the Boone County Public Library since 2008.

Melba Trujillo is a library assistant at a children's hospital and a volunteer librarian at a Cristo Rey school. She taught English as a new language at a public elementary school in Dade County, Florida, before becoming an elementary school teacher. She has a bachelor's degree in elementary education and middle school mathematics from the University of Miami and a master's degree in library and information studies from the University of Alabama.

Kacy Vega is a lead graduate advisor in the Jacobs School of Engineering at the University of California, San Diego and serves as a proud volunteer for Birch Aquarium at Scripps Institution of Oceanography. Previously, pursuing her passion for and focus on STEM-oriented programs for youth, she managed a family literacy program and the children's services department for Union County Public Library in Monroe, North Carolina. She has contributed feature articles for *Raising Arizona Kids* magazine as well as children's book reviews for Mamiverse.com and the REFORMA Newsletter.

Kelly Von Zee is the community engagement department head at the Addison (Illinois) Public Library. She has been teaching bilingual early childhood classes in public libraries for over four years and is the author of the blog *Bilingual Storytime* (http://bilingualstorytime.org). Her work includes providing relevant services and programs for Spanish-speaking families.

Index

Titles of books and CDs are shown in italic.
Titles of rhymes and songs are shown in quotes.
English and Spanish articles are ignored in alphabetization.

A

ABC Fiesta (Mister G), 73, 75
ABC Music app, 117
"Ábranlas, ciérrenlas," 77
Abuelita fue al mercado (Blackstone), 119
Abuelo (Dorros), 69
activities. *See* extension activities
Ada, Alma Flor, 59, 78, 84, 91, 103–104, 107, 122
"Adiós" (Manners), 70, 74
"Adiós" (Maria Fernanda y Sus Amigos), 110, 129
"Adiós" (Spanish Together), 106
"Adiós, amigos" (Feldman), 90
"Adiós, amigos" (Orozco), 93, 100, 116, 120
advertising, 18–20
age ranges, templates for, 42–48
El agua rueda, el agua sube (Mora), 110–111
altar activity, 129–130
Amado, Elisa, 100, 112
Américas Award, 28
"Un amigo me enseñó" (Babyradio), 84, 87
Amo nuestra tierra (Martin and Sampson), 106
Anaheim Libraries, 134
Anaya, Jorge, 80, 93, 95, 102, 107, 112–113, 118
Animal Sort activity, 100
Animalitos program, 84–87
APPitic, 57
apps, 50–62, 101, 117, 120, 130

Argueta, Jorge, 73–74, 112
Arlington County Library, 135
Arroz con leche (Argueta), 73–74
Arroz con leche (Delacre), 74
¡Arroz con leche! program, 72–75
"Aserrín aserrán," 103–104
Association for Library Service to Children (ALSC), 50, 59, 79
audio recordings, creating, 55
awards, children's literature, 28

B

babies, programs for, 43–45, 47, 75–83
The Baby Chicks Sing (Hall and Syverson-Stork), 54
Babyradio, 84, 87
Baby's First Songs in Spanish, 73
"El baile de los manos" (Anaya), 95
Baile y canto (Maria Fernanda y Sus Amigos), 108, 110, 113, 128–129
Bajo el mar program, 108–111
Bajo las olas 1, 2, 3 (Knox), 108
Bandcamp website, 98
Barchas, Sarah, 99
Barner, Bob, 128
Basho and Friends, 115
beanbags, 103–104
Beaton, Clare, 100
¡Bebés juguetones! programs, 75–83
Belpré, Pura, 3–6, 9n2, 28
Bertrand, Diane Gonzales, 69
best practices, 29–30, 43f
bibliographies, 133–146
Bilingual Songs for Children (Rosie and Andy), 125

Bilingual Storytime website, 137
bilingual storytimes
    age ranges of, 42–48
    for babies, 43–45, 47, 75–83
    digital media use in, 49–62, 101, 117, 120, 130
    early literacy emphasis of, 36–38, 43–45, 60–62, 134–136
    for families, xii, 47, 68–75, 114–131
    frameworks for, 37f, 39–42
    myths about, 7–8
    need for, x–xi, 3–4, 5–7, 35–39
    non-Spanish-speakers and, 6, 7–8, 25–34
    for preschoolers, 46–47, 95–114
    program titles for, 19f
    templates for, 45–48, 55
    for toddlers, 45–46, 47, 84–94
bilingualism, supporting, 37f–39
Bilingüitos programs, 92–94, 118–121
Blackstone, Stella, 100, 119
Blagojevic, Bonnie and Ana, 60
La Bloga website, 138
Los Bloguitos website, 138
Los bolsillos saltarines (Mora), 89
Book Day, 59, 95, 137
Book Fiesta (Mora), 95, 98
books, bilingual and Spanish-language
    awards for, 28
    circulation of, 12, 27
    cost of, 8
    cultural authenticity in, 6–7, 26, 28

books, bilingual and Spanish-language (*continued*)
  for English-language storytimes, 144–154
  selection criteria for, 28
Boone County Public Library, 20–22, 114
The Bossy Gallito (González), 126–128
Bouncing Babies! programs, 75–83
Bracegirdle, P.J., 130
Bright with Colors (Diaz), 124
Brooklyn Public Library, 83, 135
Brown, Monica, 97, 115, 117
Brown Bear, Brown Bear, What Do You See? (Martin), 122
Browne, Anthony, 126
"Buenos días," 84
"Buenos días amiguitos" (Anaya), 102, 118

C

Calavera abecedario (Winter), 130
Calderón, Anne, 61
Call Me Tree (Gonzalez), 106
Campoy, F. Isabel, 78, 83–84, 91, 103–104, 122
"Canción de despedida," 86
"Canción de nombres," 92
"Candombe de las despedidas" (Canticuénticos), 97–98
Canetti, Yanitzia, 94, 100, 106, 110, 119
Canta, Rana, canta (Rosales-Yeomans), 91
Cantaba la rana (Ruesga), 79
¡Cantamos cuentos! program, 114–117
Canticuénticos, 97–98
¡Cantos! ¡Cuentos! ¡Juegos! program, 95–98
"El caracol y la ratoncita," 78–79
case studies, 20–22, 33, 58
A Cat and a Dog (Masurel), 87
The Cazuela That the Farm Maiden Stirred (Vamos), 73
CDs, 139–140
Census Bureau, 13
Center for Early Literacy Learning, 135
Cha, Cha, Cha, Spanish Learning Songs (Anaya), 112
"Challenging Common Myths about Young English Language Learners" (Espinosa), 8
Charlotte Mecklenburg Library, 56, 58, 91
children
  babies, 43–45, 47, 75–83
  digital media use by, 50–55
  importance of bilingual programming for, x–xi, 5–7
  language and literacy development of, 4–5, 7, 38, 51–52

preschoolers, 46–47, 95–114
  toddlers, 45–46, 47, 84–94
Children's Day, 59, 95, 137
Children's Museum of Houston, 29, 75, 136
Children's Technology Review, 53, 57
Chile Crece Contigo, 136
"Chocolate," 92, 94, 113
circulation numbers, 12, 27
Cisneros, Sandra, 52, 71
cleanup songs, 77, 81, 119
closing songs
  "Adiós" (Manners), 70, 74
  "Adiós" (Maria Fernanda y Sus Amigos), 110, 129
  "Adiós" (Spanish Together), 106
  "Adiós, amigos" (Feldman), 90
  "Adiós, amigos" (Orozco), 93, 100, 116, 120
  "Candombe de las despedidas" (Canticuénticos), 97–98
  "Goodbye Song/Canción de despedida," 86
  "It's Time to Say Goodbye/ Es tiempo a decir adiós," 78, 83
collaboration. *See* partnerships
collections, Spanish-language, 8, 12, 27–28, 40, 51
Color Bingo activity, 123–124
Colorado Libraries for Early Literacy, 135
Colores de la vida (Weill), 122
colorín colorado (saying), 19f, 103
¡Colorín Colorado! (website), 27, 124, 136
color-themed programs, 121–124
Comienza en Casa program, 60–61, 138
community groups, partnerships with, 6, 12, 15–16, 19–20, 23, 30–31
"Community Leader Interview Guide" (Cuesta), 15
community leaders, connecting with, 14–16, 18–20, 23
"¿Cómo te llamas?," 75, 80, 115
Consortium of Latin American Studies Programs (CLASP), 28
Cosita linda (Mlawer), 126
crafts. *See* extension activities
Creepy Crawly Calypso (Langham), 116
Cubans, ix, xiii1. *See also* Latinos
"Cucú, cucú cantaba la rana" song, 89, 91
¡Cucú cuentos! program, 88–91
¡Cuéntame Cuentos! program, 98–101
Cuentos bilingües programs, 121–128
Cuentos y Más website, 136
Cuesta, Yolanda, 15
cultural authenticity, 6–7, 26, 28
Cumpiano, Ina, 93
Curly Hair, Straight Hair, 52

Currie, Robin, 94
customer service, 16–18, 20–22, 23

D

Dale, dale, dale (Saldaña), 96
"Dale, dale, dale" song, 96–97
Dalia's Wondrous Hair (Lacámara), 52
The Day of the Dead (Barner), 128
The Day of the Dead program, 128–131
DayByDayVA, 136
De colores (Diaz), 124
"De colores" song, 119, 121, 123–124
De Colores website, 138
The Dead Family (Bracegirdle), 130
Dear Primo (Tonatiuh), 71
Delacre, Lulu, 74, 127
"Descubriendo el sabor" (Naidoo and López-Robertson), 28
dessert-themed programs, 72–75
El día de los libros (Book Day), 59, 95, 137
Día de los Muertos (Thong), 129
El Día de los Muertos (Barner), 128
El Día de los Muertos program, 128–131
El día de los niños (Children's Day), 59, 95, 137
Día, 59, 95, 137
Diamant-Cohen, Betsy, 45, 61–62, 95
Días festivos program, 128–131
Diaz, David, 124
"Diez amigos" song, 126
Diez deditos de las manos y diez deditos de los pies (Fox), 83
"Diez deditos" rhyme, 76
Diez perritos (Ada and Campoy), 84
"Diez perritos" song, 85
digital media, 49–62, 101, 117, 120, 130
Digital Storytime website, 57
Diversity in Action (Día), 59, 95, 137
Diversity Programming for Digital Youth (Naidoo), 55
Doggie Opposites activity, 86
dog-themed programs, 84–87
Dole, Mayra L., 117
Domínguez, Adriana, 110, 115
Dominguez, Angela, 102
¿Dónde esta el ombliguito? (Ziegler), 81
Doodlecast app, 54
Dorn, Susy, 102
Dorros, Arthur, 69, 71
Draw and Tell app, 53
Drum, Chavi, Drum! (Dole), 117
Drum Dream Girl (Engle), 115
Dulces sueños (Mora), 70
"Dynamic Digital Día" (Naidoo), 59

E

Earlier Is Easier website, 136
Early Learning Collaborative (ELC), 53

early literacy, emphasis on, 36–38, 43–45, 60–62, 134–136
Early Literacy Programming en Español (Diamant-Cohen), 45, 62
"Elena la ballena," 109
Elya, Susan Middleton, 102
En pos de la música (Torres), 115
Engle, Margarita, 115
English speakers, native
 as storytime attendees, 7–8
 as storytime presenters, 6, 25–34
English-language storytimes
 children's books for, 144–154
 examples of, 68–75
 inclusion of Latino cultures in, 26–29
Es divertido hablar dos idiomas website, 94, 111, 137
"Es tiempo a decir adiós," 78, 83
Espinosa, Linda, 8
"Estamos contentos," 95
extension activities
 for families, 71, 74, 116, 120, 123, 127, 129
 for preschoolers, 97, 100, 103, 107, 110, 113
 for toddlers, 86, 91, 94
"Eyes and Ears," 80

F
FactFinder, 13
Familia Fun program, 68–71
families
 programs about, 68–71
 programs for, xii, 47, 68–75, 114–131
Family Time with Apps, 52
¡Fantástico! (Lucky Diaz and the Family Jam Band), 110, 129
farm-themed programs, 98–101
Feldman, Jean, 90, 98
Felt Board app, 54, 61–62, 101
Fiesta Babies (Tafolla), 76
fiesta-themed programs, 95–98
Finding the Music (Torres), 115
fingerplays, 45–46, 47, 126, 135
"Five Green and Specked Frogs," 89–90
flannelboards, 89–90, 96, 112–113, 122–123, 137
folktales, 27, 29f, 126–127
food-themed programs, 111–114
footprints activity, 71
Fox, Mem, 83
free play, 43, 45, 61, 77, 81
friendliness, importance of, 16–18
Friendship Wreath activity, 127
friendship-themed programs, 125–128
Frog Sizes activity, 91
The Frog Was Singing (Ruesga), 79
frog-themed programs, 88–91
From Here to There (Palis), 69, 77, 81, 105

"Frota tu Panza" (Mister G), 73
"El frutero" (Anaya), 112

G
Gallo (Luján), 100
El gallo de bodas (González), 126–128
games, as storytime component, 93–94, 123–124
Gathering the Sun (Ada), 107
Un gato y un perro (Masurel), 87
Los Gatos Black on Halloween (Montes), 130
Gerez, Toni de, 8
Girl Scouts of America, 126
Gomi, Taro, 127
González, Lucía, 127
Gonzalez, Maya Christina, 7, 106, 109, 123
"Good Morning," 84
"Goodbye Song," 86
Goodrich, Maria Lee, 42
Gracias (Mora), 125, 128
Grandpa Green (Smith), 105, 107
Graphite, 53, 57
Green Is a Chile Pepper (Thong), 112
Guernsey, Lisa, 50
Guevara, Beatriz, 56, 58
GuíaInfantil, 87, 91, 107
Guy, Ginger Foglesong, 85, 97

H
"Háganse nuevos amigos," 126
Hairs (Cisneros), 52, 71
Hall, Nancy Abraham, 54
Harris, Jay, 104
"H-E-L-L-O" (Palis), 105
"Hello Children," 88
"Hello Everybody," 121
"Hello Friends, Hola Amigos," 68, 72
Hello Ocean (Ryan), 110
A Hen, a Chick and a String Guitar (MacDonald), 117
Hispanic Information and Telecommunications Network, 53
Hispanic Trends Project, ix, xi, 13
Hispanics. *See* Latinos
Hit It, Hit It, Hit It (Saldaña), 96
"Hola, hola, hola" (Maria Fernanda y Sus Amigos), 128
"Hola, hola, hola" (Rosie and Andy), 125
"Hola a todos," 121
"Hola amigo" (Feldman), 98
Hola Mar (Ryan), 110
"Hola niños," 88
Holiday Celebrations program, 128–131
Holiday House website, 101
Hop, Jump (Walsh), 91
Horn Book, 57
Hot, Hot Roti for Dada-ji (Zia), 59
How Big Is a Pig? (Beaton), 100
"How Much Is That Doggie in the Window?," 86

I
I Know the River Loves Me (Gonzalez), 109
I Love Our Earth (Martin and Sampson), 106
I Love Saturdays y Domingos (Ada), 59
"I Take Out My Little Hand," 80
"If You Want to Read a Book, Clap Your Hands," 118
"If You're Happy and You Know It," 125
immersion, 7, 37f
El inesperado viaje de Mamut y Pingüino (Vicente), 119
infants, programs for, 43–45, 47, 75–83
International Children's Digital Library, 51
interviews, of community leaders, 14–15, 19–20, 23
iPads, 58
Irving, Jan, 94
It Starts at Home program, 60–61, 138
"It's Time to Say Goodbye," 78, 83

J
El jardín de abuelo (Martin), 105, 107
Jeffers, Oliver, 120
Joan Ganz Cooney Center, 49
Johnson County Library, 135
Johnston, Tony, 120
Juguemos a Cantar, 73
Jump, Frog, Jump! (Kalan), 90
Just a Minute (Morales), 130

K
Kalan, Robert, 90
Katz, Karen, 81
King County Library System, 71, 83, 104, 135
Knox, Barbara, 108

L
Lacámara, Laura, 52
Laínez, René Colato, 7, 98
Langham, Todd, 116
language acquisition, 4–5, 7–8, 38, 51–52
Lasconi, Diego, 99
Latin Baby Book Club, 139
Latinas for Latino Lit, 139
Latinos
 books by and about, 144–145
 diversity among, ix–x, xiiin1, 13
 outreach to, 11–24, 33, 36
 public library usage by, xi, 12–13
Latinos in Kid Lit, 139
Let's Sing Stories! program, 114–117
librarians
 case studies with, 20–22, 33, 58
 history as bilingual storytime providers, 3–4
 as media mentors, 50–51, 53, 62
 non-Spanish-speaking, 6, 25–34

libraries. *See* public libraries
"Limpia," 77, 81
literacy development, 4–5, 7, 51–52
Little Beauty (Browne), 126
"The Little Chicks," 99
Little Critters program, 84–87
Little Roja Riding Hood (Elya), 102
"Little Tortillas," 76
Llámame árbol (Gonzalez), 106
"Llueve" (Spanish Together), 106
López, Lillian, 6
Lost and Found (Jeffers), 120
Lucky Diaz and the Family Jam
    Band, 110, 129
Luján, Jorge, 100, 120, 124

M
MacDonald, Margaret Reed, 117
Maine Migrant Education Program,
    60, 138
"Make New Friends," 126
Making Learning Fun website, 87
Mamá Goose (Ada and Campoy), 104
Mama Lisa's World, 105, 126
Mango, Abuela, and Me (Medina), 59
Manners, Beth, 70, 74
Mano en Mano/Hand in Hand, 60,
    138
Map Making activity, 120
El maravilloso cabello de Dalia
    (Lacámara), 52
Marcuse, Aída E., 90
Maria Fernanda y Sus Amigos, 108,
    110, 113, 128–129
Maria Had a Little Llama
    (Dominguez), 102
María tenía una llamita (Dominguez),
    102
Marisol McDonald and the Clash Bash
    (Brown), 97
Marisol McDonald y la fiesta sin igual
    (Brown), 97
marketing, 18–20
Martin, Bill, 106, 122
Martin, Paulina de Aguinaco, 105
Masurel, Claire, 87, 99
Me llamo Celia (Brown), 117
media outlets, 12, 19, 23
Medina, Meg, 59
Mexicans, ix, xiiin1. *See also* Latinos
"Mi cuerpo hace música" (Sol y
    Canto), 115, 117
Mi familia calaca (Weill), 129
"Mi granja" (Barchas), 99
Mi jardín (Emberley), 107
¡Mira quien toca calipso! (Pérez), 116
Mis amigos (Gomi), 127
Mis amigos los animales (Warner),
    87, 109
Mis colores, mi mundo (Gonzalez), 123
Miss Mary Liberry, 127
Mister G, 73, 75
"Mister Sun," 122
mixed-age programs, xii, 47, 68–75,
    114–131

Mlawer, Teresa, 122, 126, 128
monolingual storytimes
    in English, 26–29, 68–75,
        144–145
    in Spanish, 36–37
Montes, Marisa, 130
The Moon Is La Luna (Harris), 104
Mora, Pat, 59, 70, 89, 95, 98, 110–111,
    113–114, 125, 128
Morales, Yuyi, 130
Mother Goose on the Loose en
    Español program, 61–62
The Mouse behind the House
    activity, 123
movement songs, 69–70, 73, 93, 95,
    106, 115, 125, 129
Mudluscious (Irving and Currie), 94
Muévete (Spanish Playtime), 119, 125
"Muévete" (Palis), 69
Mundo VeoVeo, 138
musical instrument activity, 116
music-themed programs, 114–117
¡Muu, Moo! (Ada and Campoy), 103,
    122
My Colors, My World (Gonzalez), 123
My Friends (Gomi), 127
My Garden (Emberley), 107
My Granny Went to Market
    (Blackstone), 119
My Name Is Celia (Brown), 117
My Skeleton Family (Weill), 129
My Story app, 53, 59

N
Naidoo, Jamie Campbell, xii, 98, 114,
    128
nature-themed programs, 105–107
Nemeth, Karen, 52–53, 57
networking groups, 19–20, 23
Nicomedes el pelón (Pinto and
    Chinto), 94
"Los niños cuando bailan" (Anaya),
    93
Los niños en su casa website, 107
No, No Titus! (Masurel), 99
¡No, Tito, no! (Lasconi), 99
non-Spanish speakers
    as storytime attendees, 7–8
    as storytime presenters, 6,
        25–34
Nourish Interactive website, 114

O
"Ojos, orejas," 80
Ole! Ole! Ole! (Feldman), 90, 98
"One to Five," 82
online resources. *See* websites
"Open, Shut Them," 77
opening songs
    "Buenos días amiguitos"
        (Anaya), 102, 118
    "Canción de nombres," 92
    "Good Morning/Buenos días,"
        84
    "H-E-L-L-O" (Palis), 105

"Hello Children/Hola niños,"
    88
"Hello Everybody/Hola a
    todos," 121
"Hello Friends, Hola Amigos,"
    68, 72
"Hola, hola, hola" (Maria
    Fernanda y Sus Amigos),
    128
"Hola, hola, hola" (Rosie and
    Andy), 125
"Hola amigo" (Feldman), 98
"What's Your Name?/Cómo te
    llamas?," 75, 80
Opuestos (Weill), 93
oral storytelling, 27, 59, 64n18, 101,
    126, 128
Orozco, José-Luis, 93, 100, 120,
    123–124
"Osito, Osito," 82
Oso pardo, oso pardo, ¿que ves ahí?
    (Mlawer), 122
outreach
    case studies of, 20–22, 33
    necessity of, 11–13, 36
    process of, 13–20, 22–24

P
P is for Piñata (Johnston), 120
Paka Paka website, 105, 138
Palabras por todas partes program,
    92–94
Palis, Nathalia, 69, 77, 81, 105, 129
Papá and Me (Dorros), 71
Para los Niños program, 29, 75, 136
parachute activity, 119
parents
    early literacy messages for, 44f
    empowerment of, 36–38, 40f,
        43f
partnerships
    with community groups, 6, 12,
        15–16, 19–20, 23, 30–31
    with community leaders, 14–16,
        18–20, 23
    with Spanish speakers, 6, 29–34
party-themed programs, 95–98
PBS Kids Lab, 71, 136
PBS Parents Play and Learn, 120
Peekaboo Stories! program, 88–91
Pelitos (Cisneros), 52, 71
Perdido y encontrado (Jeffers), 120
Pérez, Maria A., 116
¡Perros! ¡Perros! Dogs! Dogs! (Guy), 85
Pew Research Center, ix–xi, 13, 17f
Picky Paul website, 94
picture books
    bibliography of, 140–144
    as mirrors and windows, 26
piggyback songs, 80
"Pin Pon," 111–112, 114
The Piñata (Ruesga), 83
Piñata Confetti Math activity, 97
piñatas, 96–97
Pinterest, 137

Pinto and Chinto, 94
¡Pío Peep! (Ada and Campoy), 78
pizza activity, 112–113
play
    programs about, 75–83
    as storytime component, 43, 45, 61, 77, 81
Play in Spanish (Spanish Together), 106
Play-Doh, 110
Plaza Sésamo, 138
Pocoyo apps, 53
Los pollitos (Zapata), 54
Los Pollitos app, 54, 101
Los pollitos dicen (Hall and Syverson-Stork), 54
"Los pollitos dicen" song, 54, 99, 101
el postre-themed programs, 72–75
preschoolers, programs for, 46–47, 95–114
programs. *See* bilingual storytimes; monolingual storytimes
promotional materials, 18–20, 23
public libraries
    case studies of, 20–22, 33, 58
    customer service in, 16–18, 20–22, 23
    Latinos perceptions of, xi, 12–13, 18
    marketing of, 18–20, 23
Publishers Weekly, 57
Puerto Ricans, ix, 3–4, xiiin1. *See also* Latinos
Pura Belpré Award, 28

Q

¿Que hay en tu jardín? program, 105–107
¿Que hay para cenar? (Risk), 114
"Que llueva," 107
¿Qué puedes hacer con una paleta? (Tafolla), 74
Quinito's Neighborhood (Cumpiano), 93

R

Rahel, Evelio Mendez, 95
Reading Is Fundamental website, 79
Ready Set Kindergarten website, 83, 135
recordings, creating, 55
REFORMA, xiii, 14f, 28, 58–59, 137
restaurant activity, 113
review sources, for digital media, 53, 57
Reynolds, Christian, 33
rhymes
    for baby programs, 76–78, 80, 82
    for family programs, 122
    for preschool programs, 103
    as program theme, 102–105
    for toddler programs, 90, 92, 94
rhyming games, 94, 103–104
Rice Pudding (Argueta), 73–74

Rice Pudding! program, 72–75
Rima, rima program, 102–105
"Rimas 1" (Dorn), 102
Risk, Mary, 114
Rooster (Luján), 100
Rosales-Yeomans, Natalia, 91
Rosie and Andy, 125
Rosita y Conchita in 3D app, 130
Ruesga, Rita Rosa, 79, 83
Ryan, Pam Muñoz, 110

S

¡Sabor! Spanish Learning Songs (Anaya), 102, 113, 118
"Saco una manita," 80
Sago Mini Doodlecast app, 54
Saldaña, René, 96
Salsa (Argueta), 112
¡Salta, ranita, salta! (Marcuse), 90
Salta y brinca (Ada and Campoy), 91
Sampson, Michael, 106
San Francisco Symphony website, 116
"Sana, sana colita de rana," 90
Schachner, Judy, 26
Scherrer, Katie, xii, 68, 72, 75, 79, 84, 88, 95, 98, 114, 128, 137
Schon, Isabel, 28
School Library Journal, 57
Sea Creature Sculptures activity, 110
selection criteria, 28, 56–57
self-esteem, effects on, 4–7
"La Semilla" (Spanish Together), 106
Señor Pancho Had a Rancho (Laínez), 98, 101
sequential bilingualism, 37f
Sesame Street, 138
"Shake Them Bones" (Palls), 129
"The Sharks in the Sea," 109
"Si quieren leer un libro, aplaudir," 118
"Si tú estas contento," 125
Silva, Adriana, 20–22, 111–114, 147
Simon Says, 93
simultaneous bilingualism, 37f
Sing, Froggie, Sing (Rosales-Yeomans), 91
Skippyjon Jones (Schachner), 26
Smith, Lane, 105
Smithsonian Latino Center, 131
"The Snail and the Mouse," 78–79
Sol y Canto, 115
Somos primos (Bertrand), 69
songs
    for baby programs, 75–78, 80–83
    for cleanup time, 77, 81, 119
    for family programs, 68–70, 72–74, 115–116, 118–120, 121–123, 125–126, 128–129
    for movement activities, 69–70, 73, 93, 95, 106, 115, 125, 129
    for preschool programs, 95–97, 98–100, 102–103, 105–106, 108–110, 111–113

    for toddler programs, 84–86, 88–90, 92–93
    See also closing songs; opening songs
Songs! Stories! Games! program, 95–98
sorting activities, 97, 100
Spanish All Year Round (Spanish Together), 106
Spanish in Our Libraries website, 139
Spanish language
    collections in, 8, 12, 27–28, 40, 51
    monolingual storytimes in, 36–37
    promotional materials in, 18
    statistics on, x
    translation of, 18–19, 28, 40f, 43f
Spanish Playground website, 94, 107
Spanish Playtime, 119, 125
Spanish population. *See* Latinos
Spanish Rhyme Time program, 102–105
Spanish speakers, collaboration with, 6, 29–34
Spanish Together, 106
Sparkup tool, 54–55
specialized bilingual storytimes, 59, 63n16
staff members
    bilingualism in, 12, 15, 18, 30
    customer service by, 16–18, 20–22, 23
StoryBlocks website, 74, 94, 101, 121, 135
StoryPlace website, 58, 91
storytelling, 27, 59, 64n18, 101, 126, 120
storytime presenters, non-Spanish-speaking, 6, 25–34
    See also librarians
Storytime!/¡Cuéntame Cuentos! program, 98–101
storytimes. *See* bilingual storytimes; monolingual storytimes
students, as volunteers, 32
Stuff the Piñata activity, 96
Sunflower Storytime website, 124
Sweet Dreams (Mora), 70
Syverson-Stork, Jill, 54

T

tablets, 49, 51–54, 58, 101, 117, 130
Tafolla, Carmen, 74, 76
Tap, Click, Read (Guernsey and Levine), 61
Teachers With Apps website, 57
"Teddy Bear, Teddy Bear," 82
Tell Me a Story website, 71, 83, 104, 135
"Ten Good Friends," 126
Ten Little Fingers and Ten Little Toes (Fox), 83
"Ten Little Fingers" rhyme, 76
Ten Little Puppies (Ada and Campoy), 84

Texas State Library and Archives Commission, 137
Thanks (Mora), 125, 128
Thong, Roseanne Greenfield, 112, 129
"Tía Monica," 69–70, 71
"Los tiburones en la mar," 109, 111
tickle rhymes, 82
Tiempo de cuentos program, 111–114
Tito Puente, Mambo King (Brown), 115, 117
¡Toca, Chavi, Toca! (Dole), 117
toddlers, programs for, 45–46, 47, 84–94
Tomás Rivera Mexican American Children's Book Award, 28
Tomás Rivera Policy Institute, 18
Tonatiuh, Duncan, 71, 112
Torres, Jennifer, 115
"Tortillitas," 76
translations, accuracy of, 18–19, 28, 40*f*, 43*f*
travel-themed programs, 118–121
Trujillo, Melba, 121, 125, 147
trust, cultivating, 6, 17*f*
TumbleBooks, 51, 59

U

Under the Sea 1, 2, 3 (Knox), 108
Under the Sea program, 108–111
Uno, Dos, Tres (Canetti), 94
"Uno a cinco," 82
U.S. Census Bureau, 13
Utah State Library, 137

V

Vamos, Samantha, 73
El vecindario de Quinito (Cumpiano), 93
Vega, Kacy, 102, 105, 108, 147
Vicente, Antonio, 119
volunteers, working with, 31–32, 33
Von Zee, Kelly, 24, 41, 92, 118, 137, 147

W

Walsh, Ellen Stoll, 91
Warner, Mona, 87, 109
Washington County Cooperative Library Services, 135
Water Rolls, Water Rises (Mora), 110–111
water-themed programs, 108–111
We Are Cousins (Bertrand), 69
WebJunction, 14
websites
    for baby programs, 79, 83
    for early literacy resources, 135–136
    for family programs, 71, 75, 117, 121, 124, 127–128, 131
    for library resources, 134–135
    for planning resources, 137
    for preschool programs, 98, 101, 104–105, 107, 111, 114
    for Spanish-language resources, 138–139
    for toddler programs, 87, 91, 94
Weill, Cynthia, 93, 122, 129

What Can You Do with a Paleta? (Tafolla), 74
What Grows in Your Garden? program, 105–107
What's for Supper? (Risk), 114
"What's Your Name?" song, 75, 80
Where is Baby's Belly Button? (Katz), 81
Whistlefritz website, 98
Why Are You Doing That? (Amado), 100
Wiggling Pockets (Mora), 89
Winter, Jeanette, 130
Words Everywhere program, 92–94
Worthington Libraries, 135

Y

"Yo me llamo" (Maria Fernanda y Sus Amigos), 108
Yo sé que el río me ama (Gonzalez), 109
Young Children, New Media, and Libraries (Koester), 55
YouTube, 79, 87, 114, 117, 124, 128, 131, 134–135
Yum! ¡MmMm! ¡Que Rico! (Mora), 114

Z

Zapata, Andres, 54
Zero to Three website, 136
Zia, F., 59
Ziegler, Argentina Palacios, 81
Zubizarreta, Rosalma, 103, 107, 122